FERDINAND
AND
ISABELLA

FERDINAND AND ISABELLA

Paul Stevens

CHELSEA HOUSE PUBLISHERS
NEW YORK
NEW HAVEN   PHILADELPHIA

EDITOR-IN-CHIEF: Nancy Toff
EXECUTIVE EDITOR: Remmel T. Nunn
MANAGING EDITOR: Karyn Gullen Browne
COPY CHIEF: Juliann Barbato
PICTURE EDITOR: Adrian G. Allen
ART DIRECTOR: Giannella Garrett
MANUFACTURING MANAGER: Gerald Levine

Staff for FERDINAND AND ISABELLA:

SENIOR EDITOR: John W. Selfridge
ASSISTANT EDITORS: Kathleen McDermott, Bert Yaeger
EDITORIAL ASSISTANT: Scott Ash
COPY EDITORS: Michael Goodman, Ellen Scordato
ASSOCIATE PICTURE EDITOR: Juliette Dickstein
PICTURE RESEARCHER: Ann Levy
SENIOR DESIGNER: Debby Jay
ASSISTANT DESIGNER: Jill Goldreyer
PRODUCTION COORDINATOR: Joseph Romano
COVER ILLUSTRATION: © Michael Garland

CREATIVE DIRECTOR: Harold Steinberg

First Printing

1   3   5   7   9   8   6   4   2

Library of Congress Cataloging in Publication Data

Stevens, Paul. FERDINAND & ISABELLA

(World leaders past & present)
Bibliography: p.
1. Ferdinand V, King of Spain, 1452–1516—Juvenile
literature. 2. Isabella I, Queen of Spain, 1451–1504—
Juvenile literature. 3. Spain—History—Ferdinand and
Isabella, 1479–1516—Juvenile literature. 4. Spain—Kings
and rulers—Biography—Juvenile literature. [1. Ferdinand V,
King of Spain, 1452–1516. 2. Isabella I, Queen of Spain,
1451–1504. 3. Kings, queens, rulers,
etc.] I. Title. II. Title: Ferdinand and Isabella. III. Series:
World leaders past & present.
DP163.5.S74   1988   946′.03′0922 [B] [920]   87-20822

ISBN 0-87754-523-5

Contents

ADENAUER

ALEXANDER THE GREAT

MARC ANTONY

KING ARTHUR

ATATÜRK

ATTLEE

BEGIN

BEN-GURION

BISMARCK

LÉON BLUM

BOLÍVAR

CESARE BORGIA

BRANDT

BREZHNEV

CAESAR

CALVIN

CASTRO

CATHERINE THE GREAT

CHARLEMAGNE

CHIANG KAI-SHEK

CHURCHILL

CLEMENCEAU

CLEOPATRA

CORTÉS

CROMWELL

DANTON

DE GAULLE

DE VALERA

DISRAELI

EISENHOWER

ELEANOR OF AQUITAINE

QUEEN ELIZABETH I

FERDINAND AND ISABELLA

FRANCO

FREDERICK THE GREAT

INDIRA GANDHI

MOHANDAS GANDHI

GARIBALDI

GENGHIS KHAN

GLADSTONE

GORBACHEV

HAMMARSKJÖLD

HENRY VIII

HENRY OF NAVARRE

HINDENBURG

HITLER

HO CHI MINH

HUSSEIN

IVAN THE TERRIBLE

ANDREW JACKSON

JEFFERSON

JOAN OF ARC

POPE JOHN XXIII

LYNDON JOHNSON

JUÁREZ

JOHN F. KENNEDY

KENYATTA

KHOMEINI

KHRUSHCHEV

MARTIN LUTHER KING, JR.

KISSINGER

LENIN

LINCOLN

LLOYD GEORGE

LOUIS XIV

LUTHER

JUDAS MACCABEUS

MAO ZEDONG

MARY, QUEEN OF SCOTS

GOLDA MEIR

METTERNICH

MUSSOLINI

NAPOLEON

NASSER

NEHRU

NERO

NICHOLAS II

NIXON

NKRUMAH

PERICLES

PERÓN

QADDAFI

ROBESPIERRE

ELEANOR ROOSEVELT

FRANKLIN D. ROOSEVELT

THEODORE ROOSEVELT

SADAT

STALIN

SUN YAT-SEN

TAMERLANE

THATCHER

TITO

TROTSKY

TRUDEAU

TRUMAN

VICTORIA

WASHINGTON

WEIZMANN

WOODROW WILSON

XERXES

ZHOU ENLAI

ON LEADERSHIP
Arthur M. Schlesinger, jr.

LEADERSHIP, it may be said, is really what makes the world go round. Love no doubt smooths the passage; but love is a private transaction between consenting adults. Leadership is a public transaction with history. The idea of leadership affirms the capacity of individuals to move, inspire, and mobilize masses of people so that they act together in pursuit of an end. Sometimes leadership serves good purposes, sometimes bad; but whether the end is benign or evil, great leaders are those men and women who leave their personal stamp on history.

Now, the very concept of leadership implies the proposition that individuals can make a difference. This proposition has never been universally accepted. From classical times to the present day, eminent thinkers have regarded individuals as no more than the agents and pawns of larger forces, whether the gods and goddesses of the ancient world or, in the modern era, race, class, nation, the dialectic, the will of the people, the spirit of the times, history itself. Against such forces, the individual dwindles into insignificance.

So contends the thesis of historical determinism. Tolstoy's great novel *War and Peace* offers a famous statement of the case. Why, Tolstoy asked, did millions of men in the Napoleonic wars, denying their human feelings and their common sense, move back and forth across Europe slaughtering their fellows? "The war," Tolstoy answered, "was bound to happen simply because it was bound to happen." All prior history predetermined it. As for leaders, they, Tolstoy said, "are but the labels that serve to give a name to an end and, like labels, they have the least possible connection with the event." The greater the leader, "the more conspicuous the inevitability and the predestination of every act he commits." The leader, said Tolstoy, is "the slave of history."

Determinism takes many forms. Marxism is the determinism of class. Nazism the determinism of race. But the idea of men and women as the slaves of history runs athwart the deepest human instincts. Rigid determinism abolishes the idea of human freedom—

the assumption of free choice that underlies every move we make, every word we speak, every thought we think. It abolishes the idea of human responsibility, since it is manifestly unfair to reward or punish people for actions that are by definition beyond their control. No one can live consistently by any deterministic creed. The Marxist states prove this themselves by their extreme susceptibility to the cult of leadership.

More than that, history refutes the idea that individuals make no difference. In December 1931 a British politician crossing Park Avenue in New York City between 76th and 77th Streets around 10:30 P.M. looked in the wrong direction and was knocked down by an automobile—a moment, he later recalled, of a man aghast, a world aglare: "I do not understand why I was not broken like an eggshell or squashed like a gooseberry." Fourteen months later an American politician, sitting in an open car in Miami, Florida, was fired on by an assassin; the man beside him was hit. Those who believe that individuals make no difference to history might well ponder whether the next two decades would have been the same had Mario Constasino's car killed Winston Churchill in 1931 and Giuseppe Zangara's bullet killed Franklin Roosevelt in 1933. Suppose, in addition, that Adolf Hitler had been killed in the street fighting during the Munich *Putsch* of 1923 and that Lenin had died of typhus during World War I. What would the 20th century be like now?

For better or for worse, individuals do make a difference. "The notion that a people can run itself and its affairs anonymously," wrote the philosopher William James, "is now well known to be the silliest of absurdities. Mankind does nothing save through initiatives on the part of inventors, great or small, and imitation by the rest of us—these are the sole factors in human progress. Individuals of genius show the way, and set the patterns, which common people then adopt and follow."

Leadership, James suggests, means leadership in thought as well as in action. In the long run, leaders in thought may well make the greater difference to the world. But, as Woodrow Wilson once said, "Those only are leaders of men, in the general eye, who lead in action. . . . It is at their hands that new thought gets its translation into the crude language of deeds." Leaders in thought often invent in solitude and obscurity, leaving to later generations the tasks of imitation. Leaders in action—the leaders portrayed in this series—have to be effective in their own time.

And they cannot be effective by themselves. They must act in response to the rhythms of their age. Their genius must be adapted, in a phrase of William James's, "to the receptivities of the moment." Leaders are useless without followers. "There goes the mob," said the French politician hearing a clamor in the streets. "I am their leader. I must follow them." Great leaders turn the inchoate emotions of the mob to purposes of their own. They seize on the opportunities of their time, the hopes, fears, frustrations, crises, potentialities. They succeed when events have prepared the way for them, when the community is awaiting to be aroused, when they can provide the clarifying and organizing ideas. Leadership ignites the circuit between the individual and the mass and thereby alters history.

It may alter history for better or for worse. Leaders have been responsible for the most extravagant follies and most monstrous crimes that have beset suffering humanity. They have also been vital in such gains as humanity has made in individual freedom, religious and racial tolerance, social justice and respect for human rights.

There is no sure way to tell in advance who is going to lead for good and who for evil. But a glance at the gallery of men and women in *World Leaders—Past and Present* suggests some useful tests.

One test is this: do leaders lead by force or by persuasion? By command or by consent? Through most of history leadership was exercised by the divine right of authority. The duty of followers was to defer and to obey. "Theirs not to reason why,/ Theirs but to do and die." On occasion, as with the so-called "enlightened despots" of the 18th century in Europe, absolutist leadership was animated by humane purposes. More often, absolutism nourished the passion for domination, land, gold and conquest and resulted in tyranny.

The great revolution of modern times has been the revolution of equality. The idea that all people should be equal in their legal condition has undermined the old structure of authority, hierarchy and deference. The revolution of equality has had two contrary effects on the nature of leadership. For equality, as Alexis de Tocqueville pointed out in his great study *Democracy in America*, might mean equality in servitude as well as equality in freedom.

"I know of only two methods of establishing equality in the political world," Tocqueville wrote. "Rights must be given to every citizen, or none at all to anyone . . . save one, who is the master of all." There was no middle ground "between the sovereignty of all and the absolute power of one man." In his astonishing prediction of 20th-century totalitarian dictatorship, Tocqueville explained how the revolution of equality could lead to the *"Führerprinzip"* and more terrible absolutism than the world had ever known.

But when rights are given to every citizen and the sovereignty of all is established, the problem of leadership takes a new form, becomes more exacting than ever before. It is easy to issue commands and enforce them by the rope and the stake, the concentration camp and the *gulag.* It is much harder to use argument and achievement to overcome opposition and win consent. The Founding Fathers of the United States understood the difficulty. They believed that history had given them the opportunity to decide, as Alexander Hamilton wrote in the first Federalist Paper, whether men are indeed capable of basing government on "reflection and choice, or whether they are forever destined to depend . . . on accident and force."

Government by reflection and choice called for a new style of leadership and a new quality of followership. It required leaders to be responsive to popular concerns, and it required followers to be active and informed participants in the process. Democracy does not eliminate emotion from politics; sometimes it fosters demagoguery; but it is confident that, as the greatest of democratic leaders put it, you cannot fool all of the people all of the time. It measures leadership by results and retires those who overreach or falter or fail.

It is true that in the long run despots are measured by results too. But they can postpone the day of judgment, sometimes indefinitely, and in the meantime they can do infinite harm. It is also true that democracy is no guarantee of virtue and intelligence in government, for the voice of the people is not necessarily the voice of God. But democracy, by assuring the right of opposition, offers built-in resistance to the evils inherent in absolutism. As the theologian Reinhold Niebuhr summed it up, "Man's capacity for justice makes democracy possible, but man's inclination to injustice makes democracy necessary."

A second test for leadership is the end for which power is sought. When leaders have as their goal the supremacy of a master race or the promotion of totalitarian revolution or the acquisition and exploitation of colonies or the protection of greed and privilege or the preservation of personal power, it is likely that their leadership will do little to advance the cause of humanity. When their goal is the abolition of slavery, the liberation of women, the enlargement of opportunity for the poor and powerless, the extension of equal rights to racial minorities, the defense of the freedoms of expression and opposition, it is likely that their leadership will increase the sum of human liberty and welfare.

Leaders have done great harm to the world. They have also conferred great benefits. You will find both sorts in this series. Even "good" leaders must be regarded with a certain wariness. Leaders are not demigods; they put on their trousers one leg after another just like ordinary mortals. No leader is infallible, and every leader needs to be reminded of this at regular intervals. Irreverence irritates leaders but is their salvation. Unquestioning submission corrupts leaders and demands followers. Making a cult of a leader is always a mistake. Fortunately hero worship generates its own antidote. "Every hero," said Emerson, "becomes a bore at last."

The signal benefit the great leaders confer is to embolden the rest of us to live according to our own best selves, to be active, insistent, and resolute in affirming our own sense of things. For great leaders attest to the reality of human freedom against the supposed inevitabilities of history. And they attest to the wisdom and power that may lie within the most unlikely of us, which is why Abraham Lincoln remains the supreme example of great leadership. A great leader, said Emerson, exhibits new possibilities to all humanity. "We feed on genius. . . . Great men exist that there may be greater men."

Great leaders, in short, justify themselves by emancipating and empowering their followers. So humanity struggles to master its destiny, remembering with Alexis de Tocqueville: "It is true that around every man a fatal circle is traced beyond which he cannot pass; but within the wide verge of that circle he is powerful and free; as it is with man, so with communities."

1

The Court Appoints an Admiral

Isabella, queen of Castile, stared at the tall, gaunt man who stood before her. Christopher Columbus, or Cristóbal Colón, as he was known in Spain, was no stranger to her. He had been haunting her and her husband, King Ferdinand of Aragon, ever since he had first appeared before them in 1486. Yet she was surprised, even startled, at the changes that had come over the brash young man from the bustling merchant seaport of Genoa, Italy. She remembered him as he had been: his hair flaming red, his eyes piercing blue, his carriage bold and erect. Now, in late 1491, he showed the effects of the years spent waiting and hoping. His youthful eagerness had disappeared; he seemed to stoop ever so slightly, and his face showed an anger and bitterness she had not seen before. But his eyes still burned from an inner fire, and she perceived that this man, 40 years old and only a few months younger than she, was prouder and more arrogant than ever.

He was there to plead his case, as he had done so many times before. He believed, as did many scholars at the time, that by sailing west from Spain across the great uncharted Atlantic Ocean — the "Ocean Sea," as it was then known — one would ar-

A portrait of Christopher Columbus by Sebastiano del Piombo reflects the explorer's self-assurance and dignity. The momentous decision by Spanish monarchs Ferdinand and Isabella to sponsor Columbus's voyage west in 1492 profoundly affected not only Spain but all of Europe.

rive at Japan, then China, and, eventually, India. This was the so-called back-door-to-Asia theory, and Columbus felt that the riches and luxuries of the East were waiting for anyone bold enough to make the journey west. He called his plan the "Enterprise of the Indies."

Columbus began to speak. In his words he held out the lure of untold riches that would belong to Spain if only Her Majesty would support his plan — a plan that seemed to consume his thoughts, night and day. Isabella replied that Fray Juan Pérez, a friar of La Rábida, had journeyed there to Santa Fé to intercede on Columbus's behalf. The friar, she explained, had expressed the utmost faith in his friend, who, he was certain, warranted the attention of the court.

Fray Juan Pérez, once the queen's confessor, was held in high esteem. He was one of the many friars, or members of a religious order, who were consid-

The young Columbus was a redheaded firebrand with an unshakable belief in his mission. He spent several years in Portugal refining his map-making skills before approaching Ferdinand and Isabella.

In the mid-15th century Henry the Navigator established an informal headquarters for maritime studies, at Sagres, Portugal. Henry's students helped make Portugal the leading nation in contemporary exploration.

ered to be true scholars of the world. They were men of letters and often the best-educated people of 15th-century Spain.

Columbus had come to know Pérez by an accident of fate. He had first presented his ideas for a new route to Asia in 1484 to King John II of Portugal. At the time, Portugal was a world leader in exploration and discovery; in fact, it was King John's great-uncle, Henry the Navigator, who started the first school of maritime sciences. At Sagres in southwestern Portugal, Henry had attracted scholars and mapmakers to plan routes and chart waters to find the shortest and fastest way to the fabled Orient. John picked up where his great-uncle had left off, and his admirals, sailing south from Portugal, "coast hugging" the huge land mass of the African continent, were reporting new discoveries constantly. So Portugal was a logical first choice to hear Columbus's Enterprise of the Indies concept.

King John II was taken with the idea but, unfor-

Columbus, with his young son, Diego, makes plans for his "Enterprise of the Indies" voyage. The adventurer could not know that he would discover a new continent; he was seeking a fast, direct route to the Orient.

tunately, not with Columbus, a young and inexperienced sailor. John had at his disposal admirals of great skill and knowledge who would be far more capable of success. Columbus was dismissed from the court, discouraged and bitterly disappointed at his shabby treatment.

Since 1476 Columbus had been charting maps in Portugal's capital city, Lisbon, where he lived with his wife and young son, Diego. After his disappointing meeting with King John, the ambitious mapmaker and his son (his wife had since died) set sail for Spain, determined to approach King Ferdinand and Queen Isabella with his theory. As their ship approached the small port of Palos, Columbus noticed a monastery situated high on a hill overlooking the water. Realizing that he would have to provide shelter for his son while he pursued his

ambition, he and Diego set out for the monastery
— Santa María la Rábida — and arrived shortly before
dusk. Columbus was greeted by the prior, Fray Juan
Pérez, and within a short time had told the clergy-
man of his mission's real intent. Pérez, taken with
the idea, offered Diego a safe place at the monastery
for as long as necessary and also furnished Columbus with a letter of introduction to Fray Antonio de
Marchena, a powerful and influential man with a
great interest in navigation and a respected repu-
tation as an astronomer. Marchena even arranged
Columbus's first meeting with Queen Isabella.

But that was five years earlier. Now, standing before the queen in 1491, Columbus feared that this
would be his last chance to secure the support of
the crown. He reminded Isabella that neither Fray
Juan Pérez nor Fray Antonio de Marchena had ever
ridiculed his ideas.

Patiently, the queen answered that she and the
king did not think his ideas absurd, either. In fact,
she said, it was they themselves who had appointed
Hernando de Talavera to head a commission to find
out whether Columbus's scheme was plausible.

Hernando de Talavera, at that time the queen's
confessor, had indeed formed a commission con-
sisting of geographers and other learned men and
had spent several years studying the concepts involved in the project. But when at last they reported
to the queen, their findings were inconclusive; in
all probability, they had, for political and economic
reasons, deferred final judgment to the crown.

Columbus was not satisfied with this explanation. He exclaimed that, surely, every philosopher
and scholar now accepted the theory that the world
was round. He claimed, as he had so often, that
between the Orient (the East) and the Occident (the
West) there lay only a small sea that could easily be
sailed. The queen, however, stood behind Talavera's
opinion: Columbus had greatly miscalculated the
distances.

Columbus became vehement. He was certain that
his study of Marco Polo (despite the early explorer's
faulty measurements) and of the Greek astronomer

The 13th-century Italian adventurer Marco Polo left a re-
cord of his extensive travels
to the East. Columbus, like
most 15th-century explor-
ers, was well acquainted with
Polo's writings, but did not
believe his geographical
calculations.

and geographer Ptolemy showed him that no extensive voyage stood between Spain and the riches of India. The journey could be accomplished in a few days' time.

This remark won him only the queen's stern rebuff. She told Columbus that the commission had found that he chose only calculations and writings that supported his purpose. Furthermore, she reminded him, five years had passed since he had first appeared before the Spanish throne, and since that time, he had enjoyed both royal courtesy and financial help.

As Columbus began to name other nations whose patronage he could seek, Isabella smiled to herself at the audacity of the haughty Columbus in issuing the veiled threat. She knew Columbus had contacted other monarchs for support, but he had met with no success. Yet Isabella well understood the consequences of delaying too long in the matter. She was aware that other countries were becoming bolder in their explorations, and she had already seen Portugal become the leader in maritime science, pressing farther and farther south with greater success each time. She felt instinctively that she should support this venture, but intellectually and, certainly, economically, she was having a hard time finding a justification for doing so.

When asked what he wished in return for braving the Ocean Sea to islands unknown, and perhaps to a mainland, Columbus stated that he wanted to be made "Admiral of the Ocean Sea" he sailed and viceroy of the islands he discovered. He also would demand one-tenth of all the precious minerals, pearls, spices, and merchandise he could transport.

The queen shook her head. Talavera had warned her that Columbus's promises and offers were vain, unrealistic, and unacceptable. Furthermore, the commission had pointed out, such a voyage, even if successful, would take three years to complete and returning would be impossible, for no ship can sail "uphill" from the bottom of the world. The time had come for the queen to close the matter, and she gravely pronounced her refusal.

Even accustomed to disappointment as he was, Columbus seemed unprepared for her rejection. Perhaps now he would have to take his plan to the French, Columbus indicated bitterly as he turned and strode from the room. He was outraged at having expended five years trying to win the Spanish throne's support only to be summarily dismissed.

Isabella watched him go, but she felt no sense of relief that the matter had ended. Something inside her made her want to encourage, even sponsor, this daring voyage. The thought of converting to Christianity the Eastern heathen greatly appealed to the devout queen. But the timing was wrong, for she and Ferdinand were consumed with a more important goal—the unification of Spain.

The queen and king, preoccupied as they were

Columbus's map of the world shows how little 15th-century Europeans really knew of geography. Europe and Africa are well represented, but Asia is grossly distorted. North and South America were unknown at the time.

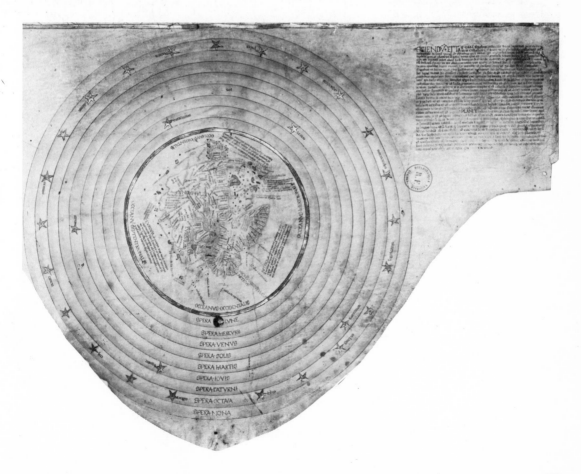

Columbus presents his argument for a new route to the Indies to Queen Isabella. The explorer first approached the Spanish rulers in 1486 but did not receive their support until five years later.

with their domestic struggle, had little time for the shaky proposal of this daydreaming sailor from Genoa. Ferdinand, especially, had been singularly unimpressed by the boastful adventurer. Isabella was intrigued; there was no doubt of that. But what she did not — could not — tell Columbus was that even if Talavera and the commission had endorsed his plan wholeheartedly, Spain could not afford to underwrite the venture. The truth was, the royal treasury had been depleted by the long and costly war they were now engaged in against the Moors, or Muslim Arabs, of southern Spain. A financial recovery would take years. As Columbus made his angry departure, Isabella wished she could have given him a different answer. It seemed, however, that fate was about to offer her the opportunity.

Word spread quickly through the court that the queen had sent Columbus on his way. Luis de Santángel, Ferdinand's keeper of the privy purse, urgently hurried to Isabella. Santángel, a trusted adviser and codirector of the Spanish state police, was more than a little upset. He had become a friend of Columbus and had seen many benefits in supporting the proposed undertaking. He requested permission to speak to the queen.

Santángel expressed astonishment to Isabella that she would give in to doubts concerning Columbus's proposal. The mission, he argued, was virtually certain to yield great wealth for Spain while exalting God and the church.

The queen was taken by surprise. Never before had she heard anyone of so high a rank and station argue so positively on behalf of Columbus. Moreover, Santángel warned, if any other prince should successfully undertake such a venture, damage to Her Majesty's crown would be easy to see. Santángel paused to let his meaning sink in. Isabella pondered once more the risk of turning her back on the possible success of so great an enterprise and the increased prestige it would bring to Spain. But then again, what if Columbus failed?

As if anticipating her question, Santángel suggested that even if Columbus were to fail, Isabella's generosity and courage would be recognized. To Santángel there was much to gain and little to lose by helping the sailor.

Seeing that his arguments were beginning to persuade the queen, Santángel pressed his case. He was certain that the dispirited Columbus could not have gotten far on his mule. A horseman could be sent to fetch him. More importantly, as keeper of the privy purse, he was confident that he could find a way to finance this expedition.

A rider was dispatched, and King Ferdinand was asked to join his queen. Santángel outlined his plan before them both. He reminded the monarchs that the other director of the state police, Francesco Pinelli, was a banker in Seville. Pinelli, originally from Columbus's home city of Genoa, shared Santángel's enthusiasm for the voyage. And, through his banking connections Pinelli was willing to guarantee a loan to the crown to help finance Columbus. Santángel, for his part, pointed out an overlooked debt to the crown. Palos, on the southern coast of Castile,

> *What made Isabel[la] change her mind, in this brief and trembling interlude when the whole fate of the world, when all modern history hung in the balance? . . . Probably in the end it was her own unconquerable admiration of the man and her faith in his vision.*
> —TOWNSEND MILLER historian, on Isabella's reconsideration of Columbus's proposal

had been found guilty of smuggling, and a fine had been levied against it that had gone uncollected. It was decreed that Palos owed the crown "three months' service, and two caravels" (small, fast-sailing ships). When taken together, the loan and the fine would be almost enough.

Ferdinand promptly suggested that Columbus should pay the rest. The king had considered the Enterprise of the Indies a flight of fancy. He was a practical man, at his best with diplomatic matters and military affairs. Indeed, the only reasons he could find to go along with this ludicrous journey were economic and military. Columbus's promises of gold and other riches were intriguing enough, but if the sailor could find the "back door to Asia," Ferdinand could use it to his advantage. The war with the Moors was not yet over, but the king was already considering his newest threat — the Muslim Ottoman Turks, who had conquered the eastern

A fanciful depiction of Columbus's 1492 departure. Columbus was 40 when he sailed west for the first time, having spent most of his life seeking a sponsor.

Mediterranean seaboard. If his army could sail west to Asia and then cross the continent on foot, he could trap the Turks in a pincer movement and defeat them.

A short while after Santángel's plea, Columbus appeared before Ferdinand and Isabella. Bewildered and confused, he was as arrogant as ever — much to Ferdinand's annoyance.

However, it was Isabella who spoke. She calmly pointed out that the seemingly outlandish proposal was being seriously considered once more. But, she asserted, because there was no certainty of success, Columbus must bear one-eighth of the expense for fitting out his ships.

Columbus immediately assented. Yet, without hesitation, he demanded in return one-eighth of the profits for himself. He had no idea where his contribution would come from. He would borrow it from friends, beg it, or steal it, if necessary, but he would find the money.

In April 1492 the agreements were finally sealed, and Cristóbal Colón became admiral of the Ocean Sea and viceroy and governor-general of lands not yet discovered. When he departed in August, he carried with him Isabella's vision of an expanding, crusading Spain. No one could have foreseen that this strange turn of events, spearheaded by the quiet, conservative keeper of the privy purse, would help transform the splintered, provincial country of Spain into one of the most powerful nations the world had ever known.

In this reconstruction of Columbus's cabin aboard the *Santa Maria* are his sword (left) and the royal flag of Ferdinand and Isabella, for whom he would claim all new lands he discovered.

2
The Secret Wedding

The Iberian Peninsula is bordered on the east and south by the Mediterranean Sea. At its southernmost point it is connected by the Strait of Gibraltar to the Atlantic Ocean, which gives the country of Portugal most of the western coastline. To the north lies the Bay of Biscay; to the northeast is the peninsula's only connection to land, the Pyrenees Mountains, over which one can travel to reach France. From earliest history, many different peoples have settled in this region, resulting in a mixture of races and cultures. The Iberians from northern Africa, the Phoenicians from what is now Lebanon, Germanic and Celtic invaders from central Europe, the Greeks, the Carthaginians from present-day Tunisia, and the Romans have all occupied the area.

The closest Spain ever got to becoming a unified country was as a province within the Roman Empire. The Romans brought with them certain unifying principles, such as the same Latin-based language and Roman law, customs, and social mores. Spain was part of the Roman Empire until the 5th century, when the Germanic tribe known as the Visigoths conquered much of the peninsula. Then, early in the 8th century, the Muslims of Arabia, completing an explosive dynastic expansion

The furtively contracted marriage was to prove one of the most important events in Spanish history.
—MELVEENA MCKENDRICK
biographer, on the union of
Ferdinand and Isabella

Isabella was the only daughter of King John II of Castile. With an older half brother, Henry, and her own brother, Alfonso, in line for the throne, Isabella was never trained to rule. But her intelligence and determination made up for her lack of royal education.

This fragment of a 2nd-century Roman mosaic from Spain indicates one of the many cultures the Iberian Peninsula has absorbed. Spain has been host to such different peoples as Germanic tribes from central Europe, Greeks, and Muslim Arabs.

across North Africa, crossed the Strait of Gibraltar and took control of most of Spain. The Muslim conquerors of Spain and North Africa are commonly called Moors.

All over Spain, pockets of resistance soon formed to fight the Moors; the first major victory over the conquerors was at Covadonga, in the far north of Spain, in 718. Although divided by provincial loyalties and different customs the rebels shared one important feature — Christianity — and their struggle became a holy war. Over the next 500 years, the Christians nibbled away at the Moors' holdings, a process that became known as the Reconquest of Spain. On July 16, 1212, a Christian army under King Alfonso VIII of Castile won a decisive battle at Las Navas de Tolosa in Andalusia, the southwestern region of Spain. This gave the Christian resistance the momentum it needed, and in 1236 Ferdinand III, known as Saint Ferdinand, king of Castile and León (he had united the two kingdoms), captured Córdoba. When Ferdinand captured Seville in 1248, the two major cities in Andalusia belonged again to the Christians. The Moors were driven all the way down to the southern coastline of the peninsula, forced to cede all of their territory except the small kingdom of Granada.

At the turn of the 15th century, the Iberian Peninsula was divided into five sectors. There were three large Christian kingdoms: Portugal, which lay along the western coast; Castile, the largest of all, which stretched from the Bay of Biscay down through the center of the peninsula; and Aragon, which bordered the Mediterranean to the east and the Pyrenees to the north. The tiny Christian kingdom of Navarre nestled in the north between Castile and Aragon. Finally, there was Granada, still occupied by the Moors, who had fought fiercely throughout the 14th century to retain it.

In the western part of Spain, King John II of Aragon had worked hard to unify his domain. By 1450 Aragon was actually composed of Aragon itself, Catalonia, and Valencia. Thus his country had an impressive amount of coastline, which John used to great advantage by developing international trade and exploiting his connections to the dependent Aragonese territories of the Balearic Islands, just off the coast of Aragon, and the kingdoms of Naples, Sardinia, and Sicily. Aragon's Italian lands had been acquired over a period of time dating back to the 13th century. Because Aragon depended heavily on these overseas ties and the commerce they generated, a kind of parliamentary government had developed in which the principal political force was a strong merchant class. By contrast, Castile had focused its efforts inward to reconquer the Spanish provinces. The kingdom was dominated by rich nobles who were, in effect, independent warlords, each with his own standing army and local rule.

King John was an intelligent and clever man. He

This map of 15th-century Iberia shows the primary divisions of the peninsula. The kingdom of Castile occupied the largest area but was politically fragmented. Aragon was stronger, more consolidated, and better ruled.

had married his first wife, Blanche of Navarre, to unify Aragon and Navarre. They had three children: Blanche of Aragon, Eleanor of Navarre, and, in 1421, Charles of Viana, who was heir to both crowns. When Blanche of Navarre died, John remarried, choosing Juana Enriquez, a young Castilian noblewoman, as his bride.

On March 10, 1452, Juana gave birth to a son, Ferdinand II of Aragon. Young Ferdinand soon became the couple's favorite; King John saw in him many of the qualities that he himself possessed, and the young and ambitious Juana saw in her son a means to secure her family's wealth and power, by making the boy heir to the throne in place of Charles. So John and Juana contrived to alienate Charles from the court, and in 1460 they had him put in prison, proclaiming Ferdinand to be the true heir.

This action caused quite an outrage within the parliamentary government as well as with the general population. Opposition from the Catalans was particularly strong; an old dynastic rivalry between Aragon and Catalonia made the Catalans fear losing even more power to the new Castilian queen and her supporters. Indeed, the pressure was so severe that in 1461 John was forced to release Charles from prison. Within that same year, however, Charles, at the age of 40, died of what the family said was a fever. Although charges of poisoning were voiced, nothing to that effect could be proved. All the while, Aragon had been attempting to subdue the rebels in Catalonia; the untimely death of Charles served only to stiffen the opposition, and it was not until 1472, more than 10 years later, that Aragon completely subdued Catalonia and Ferdinand became undisputed heir to the throne.

Isabella followed an even more difficult path to attain the status of heir to the throne of Castile. Her father, King John II of Castile, married Maria of Aragon, sister of John II of Aragon. Clearly, this was a political marriage intended to produce a son who could inherit the thrones of both Aragon and Castile.

Unlike his counterpart in Aragon, John II of Castile cared little for affairs of state, occupying himself with dancing, jousting, and playing the lute while his powerful adviser Alvaro de Luna ran the country. The Castilian nobles seized upon this obvious sign of weakness. They greedily gobbled up land and wealth, growing more powerful at the expense of the king. Castile, instead of becoming more unified, splintered into political factions, each vying for more and more control.

John and Maria had a son, Henry IV, the heir to the throne of Castile, who would later prove as unable to govern as his father. When Maria died, Alvaro de Luna arranged a new marriage for John to Isabella of Portugal, believing that he could control Isabella as he did John, but the new queen resented the minister's arrogance and power and plotted his downfall. Within two years Luna was arrested and executed in Valladolid in June 1453. Isabella of Portugal had two children, Isabella of Castile, born on April 22, 1451, and Alfonso, born two years later.

Unlike his future wife, Ferdinand of Aragon received an education with a view to his eventual succession to the throne. Even as a young prince he showed a great deal of political, diplomatic, and military skill.

The bleak castle at Arévalo was home to young Isabella. Exiled from the royal court by Henry IV in 1454, Isabella spent a lonely childhood at the castle, where she was given the rudiments of education by local priests.

In 1454 King John II of Castile died. He had done a poor job as king, and he knew it; with his last words he regretted that he "had not been born the son of a mechanic, instead of king of Castile." Henry IV ascended to the throne. Although he had shown promise as a youth — even earning the epithet "the Liberal" for his generous donations — as king, Henry mismanaged the country badly. Rebellions broke out, the crime rate soared, court corruption multiplied, and the treasury was drained, a financial condition he sought to counter by imposing higher taxes and debasing the currency, which led only to enormous inflation.

One of Henry's first acts was to exile Isabella of Portugal and her two children to a small castle in Arévalo, in the remote heart of Castile, where they would live in seclusion for the next 15 years. Young Isabella thus was not brought up to the expectations of a ruler, as Ferdinand was. She was given the rudiments of education by clergymen who traveled from Ávila, but she learned primarily sewing and embroidering and the general household skills no-blewomen were expected to have. One skill she acquired at Arévalo, however, would later prove of immense importance: She learned to ride and showed a great talent for horsemanship. But Isabella must have led a lonely childhood, for her royal blood prevented her from associating with the town's children, and she was exiled from the court, where she would have found suitable companions.

After a 12-year childless marriage to Blanche of Aragon, Henry had the union annulled, and in 1455 he married Juana of Portugal. When another six years passed without the birth of a child, Henry became something of a laughingstock and was called Henry the Impotent. In 1462, when Juana of Portugal bore a daughter, Juana, it was widely believed that she was really the illegitimate daughter of Henry's favorite in court, Beltrán de la Cueva. The poor girl became known for the rest of her life as La Beltraneja, and when Henry tried to declare her the rightful heir to the throne, civil war broke out. In 1465 the nobles refused to acknowledge Henry as king and swore allegiance to his half brother, Alfonso, who was only 12 years old.

At the same time, Isabella, now 14, was facing considerable pressure from Henry to accept as husband King Alfonso V of Portugal, who was the brother of Henry's wife, Juana, and twice Isabella's age. Isabella, however, showed an extraordinary flair for both politics and diplomacy by declaring, "The infantas [princesses] of Castile could not be disposed of in marriage without the consent of the nobles of the realm." The clever girl knew that Henry could never gain the approval of the nobles, who were rebelling against him. It seems that the resolute Isabella had by this time already decided she would marry Ferdinand of Aragon.

In 1468 Alfonso, not yet 15, was found dead in his bed. As a result, Isabella and Juana la Beltraneja, each the focus of different supporters, became rivals for the throne. Once again, Isabella displayed her political astuteness by refusing to challenge Juana directly; instead, she arranged a reconcilia-

If ever it was permitted among mortal men to say that one spirit might infuse two bodies, these are two bodies by which one spirit and one will are ruled.
—PETER MARTYR
diplomatic representative of the Spanish court, on Ferdinand and Isabella

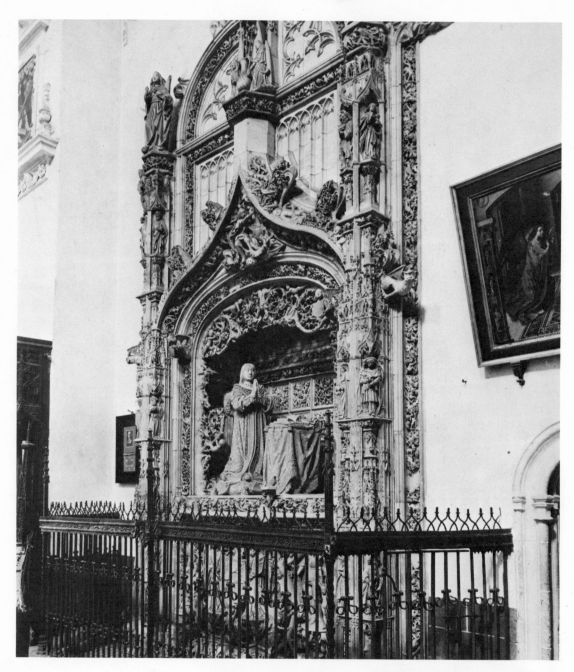

The tomb of Alfonso, Isabella's brother, who died in 1468. His sudden death made Isabella a possible heir to the throne, since many Castilians refused to recognize Juana la Beltraneja as Henry's legitimate daughter.

tion with her half brother. She negotiated to have Henry name her heir to the thrones of Castile and León, and Henry also promised not to force her to marry against her wishes. In return, she promised not to marry without his consent. Suddenly, Isabella became a real political prize. She received marriage proposals from as far away as England, but she had already decided on Ferdinand of Aragon, even though she had never met him. She gathered what knowledge she could and learned as much about him as she needed to know.

Ferdinand was young, charming, handsome, and had the makings of a fine leader. He was shrewd and sometimes devious; he was an experienced soldier and an excellent hunter; he enjoyed jousting and was a skillful horseman. Above all, he was known for his ability to remain fair and even-tempered. All these qualities pleased her, but what convinced her was the notion that marriage to Ferdinand would at last bring about the unification of Aragon and Castile. Perhaps someday they could rule all of a united Spain.

When Henry threatened to imprison Isabella if she did not marry Alfonso of Portugal, the determined infanta took this as a breach of their contract and declared their agreement void. Isabella then sent a marriage agreement to John II of Aragon, informing him that she would accept Ferdinand. The wily old king signed the document immediately. Because of the danger of Henry discovering and preventing the union, all the parties involved kept it a matter of great secrecy.

Henry IV notwithstanding, there was another problem that had to be overcome in order for the marriage to take place. Ferdinand and Isabella were cousins, descended from the same great-grandparents. According to the laws of the Catholic church, they could not be married without a dispensation — written permission — from the pope. King John of Aragon knew that there was not enough time to dispatch an official envoy to the Vatican to receive such a blessing; Henry would discover the plot long before such a journey was completed. Fortunately,

HENRI IV.
Roy de Castille.
Mort a Ségovie en Decembre 1474.

Henry IV was reconciled to Isabella when she promised not to marry without his consent and he, in turn, officially recognized her as heir. Isabella even returned to the royal court, but factions supporting Henry's daughter worked against her.

When Isabella became heir to the Castilian throne her political value as a bride soared. Marriage proposals came from rulers throughout Europe, including England's Edward IV, shown here. Isabella, however, had already decided on her cousin Ferdinand.

Alfonso Carrillo, archbishop of Toledo, understood the urgency of the situation and, together with King John, forged a papal bull stating that Ferdinand was allowed to marry his cousin. The real dispensation would arrive later. Isabella, however, because of her strict devotion, was not told of the deception. Carrillo showed her the forged paper and announced that there was nothing standing in the way of the marriage.

On a cold night in early October 1469, a small band of noblemen dressed as merchants set out from Aragon to cross the mountains to the town of Valladolid in Castile. The young man who waited on them was 17-year-old Ferdinand, who had assumed this disguise to protect his mission, for he was finally on his way to meet and marry Isabella. If the group was discovered, it would be in hostile territory, unable to count on aid from Aragon.

At length they approached the walled and fortified eastern Castilian town of Burgo de Osma, situated in a strategic position overlooking the Duero River. In a challenge from the guards on the battlements it became clear that the merchant band was not what it claimed to be, and one of the guards threw a large stone, just missing the future king of Aragon. The Aragonese noblemen had to reveal their identity, but fortunately, Burgo de Osma supported Isabella's claim to the throne. Ferdinand and his men were welcomed and sheltered in the town. The town mayor led the escort party that guided the prince and his guards to Dueñas, a town in León, where they were delivered into the hands of a group of rich and powerful noblemen who were supporters of Isabella. These men protected the travelers for the next several days as they recovered from the rigors of their long and difficult journey. On October 15, 1469, the noblemen escorted the young prince across the final 18 miles to Valladolid, where he was introduced to 18-year-old Isabella for the first time.

Four days later Ferdinand stood beside the Castilian infanta about to become his wife. He gazed at her almost as if she were a stranger; he saw that she was attractive but not pretty, and slightly pudgy

Ferdinand passed this 13th-century castle at Burgo de Osma en route to his secret wedding with Isabella in October 1469. The Aragonese prince traveled incognito to avoid detection by Henry's supporters.

but sweet. She had reddish-blond hair and had inherited the striking blue-green eyes sometimes found in descendants of the House of Trastámara. Although Ferdinand belonged to the same house, he was dark, with brown eyes and black hair. Just by talking with her for a short time when they had met, Ferdinand realized that here was a woman who, although still so young, was intelligent, dignified, and above all, understood that the first duty of a queen was not to herself but to her people.

Carrillo, the archbishop of Toledo, performed the simple ceremony in the small house in Valladolid. Despite the secrecy surrounding the wedding, the celebration festivities lasted a full week, a fact that did not much please the couple because they had to borrow money to pay for it. But the greatest surprise was yet to come, for although this was a political marriage, it would turn out to be a very happy one for Ferdinand and Isabella. It would also prove to be a momentous union for Spain.

3

Castile Must Be Saved

The wedding of Ferdinand and Isabella in 1469 did not end with the joyful couple riding off into the sunset to live happily ever after. Quite the opposite, for both of them knew that their marriage was to be a working relationship and that they would enjoy little or no peace for years to come.

Aragon, the kingdom Ferdinand would inherit, was in reasonably good condition, thanks to the efforts of his father, King John II. Castile, however, was a disaster. In its medieval chaos justice was a meaningless word, because the country had no single set of laws. Each province, often each town or village, had its own statutes or codes, so that what was legal in one village could be illegal in the next. The nobles, or grandees as they were sometimes called, held all the power. They would set the laws, often arbitrarily, in order to secure or reinforce their own authority. Groups called *hermandades* — brotherhoods — formed in some towns to enforce some kind of lawfulness, but they were subject to no central authority and degenerated into mere vigilante bands. Even worse, in much of the countryside lawlessness reigned, for most of the grandees did not maintain a police force large enough to enforce what few laws there were.

At the same time, the royal coffers were practically empty, because the grandees collected and kept for

The bitter war of succession . . . was a critical point in Spanish, and even in world, history.
—MELVEENA MCKENDRICK biographer, on the war for Castile

The Castillo de los Templarios in León is one example of the source of Castile's name — the land of castles. To establish her claim to the throne Isabella had to win the loyalty of the powerful nobles who occupied such fortified castles throughout Castile.

The effigy of a knight of Santiago portrays him in armor, holding his sword. Three orders of knighthood in Castile provided the independent nobles with a way to unite against a central authority to protect their own interests.

themselves the revenues imposed upon the people. This deprived the throne of much-needed income and meant that most of the population was desperately poor. With each year, the nobles grew a little stronger at the expense of the king. Henry IV allowed this predicament to continue. He even permitted the grandees to build and operate their own mints for printing money, with the result that Castile did not even have a common currency.

The grandees also controlled the *Consejo Real*, or Royal Council, a body formed to govern the entire kingdom. Not surprisingly, each of the grandees on the council sought to improve his own position by passing laws that had little or nothing to do with the improvement of Castile as a whole. Consequently, there was virtually no communication between the various regions of the country, roads and bridges were practically nonexistent, and people were subject to the whims of the local grandees. Twice a year there were gigantic drives that saw thousands of sheep — a Castilian economic mainstay — sweep across much of the fertile land, grazing indiscriminately upon anything that was growing, including the crops planted by farmers. Without roads or predetermined trails to follow, the herds destroyed much of the food the country needed.

Even if the drives proved successful, much of the prized wool was wasted, for Castile had not done very well in establishing its international trade. The Atlantic coastline and the best trade routes belonged to Portugal. Much of the coastline to the south, bordering on the Mediterranean and the Strait of Gibraltar — another access route to the Atlantic — belonged to Granada, the small country controlled by the hostile Moors.

The nobles had contrived another way to maintain their control over Castile. They had created three private societies called orders of knighthood. The three orders — Santiago, Calatrava, and Alcántara — were enormously wealthy and powerful, and it was the ultimate desire of every nobleman to belong to one of them. These societies had been formed by the aristocracy for nothing more than self-aggrandizement, and they eventually became formidable adversaries of the throne because they served to unite the aristocracy against the king in the protection of its own interests.

In addition to the nobility there was another group that had begun to exercise considerable control in Castilian affairs. The Catholic church, perceiving the weakness of the king, had begun to exert its own influence over the country. In years past, the desires of the crown had held great weight in the appointments of high-ranking church officials. But with the crown's power on the wane, papal control increased steadily to the point where many ecclesiastical appointments were given to foreign church representatives who had never been in Spain. Their level of scholarship was low, which proved harmful to the communities they served, for the church had always been the primary source of teachers, scholars, and scientists. Many of them were easily corrupted by unchecked power and the money given to them by the governing nobles, who sensed an opportunity to exert their control over the church.

These, then, were the main problems confronting Ferdinand and Isabella: the decentralization of the government, which had resulted in a large number of regional power bases belonging to the grandees, and the loss of control over the Catholic church, the consequences of which included degradation and corruption. It was not a pleasant way to start a marriage in which the ultimate goal was to unify Spain, especially when neither spouse was, technically, ruler of his or her respective country. True, Ferdinand had been named heir to the throne of Aragon, but his father was still king. Of course, nobody could agree as to who would succeed Henry IV.

Ferdinand and Isabella simply decided that they would act as if they were the true sovereigns of Castile, although, by consent, Ferdinand was never to be more than consort (that is, king in name but not in power) of Castile. This was because the couple's marriage contract stipulated that each would retain sole sovereignty — if and when that sovereignty was

Ferdinand and Isabella had to stop the great families from taking Castile's (and this meant Spain's) affairs in their own hands.
—MAURICE ROWDON
British historian

acquired — of his or her respective kingdom. The contract also specified that only a male child born to them could inherit both kingdoms to become the king of Spain.

Ferdinand and Isabella sent word to King Henry IV that they had been married and asked him for his blessing. News of the secret wedding served only to anger him. "My ministers must be consulted" was his curt response to the couple, and the king set out to destroy the union. Ferdinand and Isabella realized the precarious situation they were in and moved from Valladolid, on the open Castilian plain, to the more easily defended town of Dueñas. In this town their first child, Isabella, was born in 1470.

King Henry found an ally in King Louis XI of France, who saw the marriage as a threat to Henry's sovereignty and, therefore, to certain agreements France had made with Castile. Henry proclaimed that Isabella, by entering into an unauthorized marriage, had forfeited her right to inherit the crown. Henry designated his daughter, Juana la Beltra-

King Louis XI of France, Henry's ally, encouraged the Castilian king to disinherit Isabella for marrying Ferdinand. Henry reinstated Juana la Beltraneja as heir, but many Castilians continued to support Isabella.

A 15th-century French knight and his horse in full armor. King Louis of France seized two provinces belonging to Aragon, forcing Ferdinand to leave his new bride in order to help his father defeat the French.

This castle at Segovia was Isabella's favorite. The young princess was in Segovia when Henry IV died suddenly in 1474. Isabella immediately proclaimed herself queen of Castile, but complete control of the kingdom was yet to be won.

neja, rightful heir and announced that she would marry Louis's brother, the duke of Guyenne, to cement the relationship between Castile and France.

Louis proceeded to complicate the fortunes of Ferdinand and Isabella by annexing the northeast Aragonese territories of Roussillon and Cerdagne in the Pyrenees. Aragon now had two wars on its hands, for the revolt by the Catalonian rebels had still not been suppressed.

The proclamations issued by Henry IV disinheriting Isabella served to stir up even more internal conflicts. The nobility, already divided in its allegiance between Isabella and Henry, redoubled their feuding. Civil strife, if not actual war, broke out all over Castile. Isabella began a practice that would earn her the name of the "Traveling Queen." She rode from town to town to encourage her supporters, believing that nothing less than her personal appearance would help restore order. She was tireless in her efforts, and no journey, no matter how great the distance, could stop her crusade. It was a course of action she was to follow all her life; in fact, each of her five children was born in a different town.

Isabella's efforts brought her considerable support. The Castilian Cortes, or parliament, refused to acknowledge Juana as heir. Isabella won over many noble families who were tired of Henry's mismanagement and corruption. Andalusia in the south and the Basque region in the north came into her camp, and she even won the support of the great Mendoza family, one of the most illustrious ancient clans in Castile. In 1472, when the Catalonian rebels finally fell to Aragon, Ferdinand became the undisputed heir to the Aragonese throne.

In 1473 Henry seemed to have a change of heart and agreed to a meeting with Isabella in Segovia. He even met Ferdinand for the first time. His newfound geniality did not last, however, for in January 1474 he fell ill and accused Isabella of trying to poison him. The young couple remained in Segovia, which was fiercely loyal to Isabella, but in August Ferdinand had to leave Isabella to join his father,

King John, in the fight to win back the territory taken by France.

Suddenly, on December 11, 1474, Henry IV died in Madrid, without having named his successor to the throne. Upon receiving the news, Isabella, still in Segovia, made the most crucial decision of her life and instantly proclaimed herself queen of Castile. Two days later, in a traditional ceremony, she received homage from the people. She drew her sword, held it to the sky with its hilt upward, and led a procession to the town cathedral. The Cortes immediately swore allegiance to Isabella.

When Ferdinand received the news, he hurried to Segovia. Coming from a kingdom in which only males could inherit the throne, he was disturbed that Isabella had so forcefully assumed power, feeling that it in some way diminished his own standing in Castile. A serious rift threatened to develop between the couple as each monarch sought to define what his or her power would be in each kingdom. With Archbishop Carrillo and Cardinal Pedro González de Mendoza as mediators, Ferdinand and Isabella quickly came to an agreement. When together, they would rule equally, but Isabella would continue to have sole claim to the Castilian crown, in accordance with their marriage contract.

Isabella had in store a much more serious challenge to her crown. In May 1475, 13-year-old Juana la Beltraneja claimed the throne as Henry's rightful heir, even though many still believed her to be illegitimate. King Alfonso V of Portugal, her uncle, supported her claim because he wanted to marry her and unite Portugal and Castile, thereby cutting off Aragon from the western coastline and the Atlantic.

When Juana announced her claim to the throne, Portugal invaded Castile. Twenty thousand Portuguese troops spilled across the border and quickly established a firm hold on Castile's western border. The attacking forces halted at the town of Plasencia, where Alfonso, with a papal dispensation, married his niece Juana. The company moved on to Arévalo, where the ensuing festivities lasted for a week. The army then waited for Castilian reinforcements — the supporters of Juana la Beltraneja — at whose center was another of Henry's favorites, Diego López Pacheco, the marqués of Villena. Isabella was anguished to discover that Archbishop Carrillo, in a pique over not receiving a cardinal's hat, joined the enemy camp. Alfonso's delay, however, offered Ferdinand and Isabella the time they needed to gather troops; at the start of the war the monarchs had only 500 trained soldiers. Ferdinand rode north and west to muster men, while Isabella concentrated on Old and New Castile, where her support was strongest. The queen, who was pregnant again, rode from town to town in the scorching summer heat, bringing together everyone she could. When she suffered a miscarriage, she took only two days to recover before she resumed her riding. By July, Ferdinand and Isabella commanded an army of approximately 40,000 at Valladolid. The queen went south to set up headquarters at Tordesillas, and Ferdinand led the Castilian army west to Toro, where Alfonso had encamped. The young king's first major offensive was a demoralizing disaster; the hastily assembled and unwieldy Castilian army quickly fell apart. Clearly, a new strategy was needed.

In August the monarchs summoned the Cortes in Medina del Campo to raise money to pay the army. Isabella gratefully accepted a loan from the Castilian clergy of one-half of the silver and gold plate belonging to the Church. (The queen paid back the debt within three years.) Ferdinand reorganized and streamlined the army. He brought in the finest military strategists from Aragon. By the end of 1475, Ferdinand had retaken Zamora. The following February, Alfonso held Ferdinand at Zamora in a siege for two weeks but was unable to defeat him. With the light cavalry Isabella had obtained from Andalusia and Estremadura, raids were carried out on many Portuguese border towns. The Portuguese king was losing support rapidly; many Castilian defectors, including the repentant archbishop of Toledo, returned to Isabella.

The real turning point of the war came in March

When Isabella forcefully assumed the throne of Castile a serious rift between her and Ferdinand threatened to develop over the extent of his power in Castile. At this point, each monarch's place in the other's kingdom was carefully established.

King Alfonso V of Portugal invaded Castile in 1475 to restore the claim of Juana la Beltraneja, his niece. The four-year war was a trial by fire for Ferdinand and Isabella, who commanded only 500 soldiers at the start of the conflict.

In January 1479 Ferdinand inherited the crown of Aragon, and the now royal couple brought a successful end to the war with Portugal. The birth of a son and heir, John, the previous year offered real hope for their dream of unifying Aragon and Castile.

1476, near the town of Toro, 20 miles east of Zamora, on the Duero River. After his siege of Zamora had failed, Alfonso led his army in a retreat back to Toro, which was easily defensible. Ferdinand immediately followed the enemy, and when he found the Portuguese army encamped on the plains near the river (a grossly incompetent move on Alfonso's part), he quickly attacked. The ensuing battle was a virtual massacre, as Ferdinand's troops tore apart the helpless Portuguese.

When news of the battle reached Isabella in Tordesillas the following morning, she celebrated the great victory by walking barefoot to the monastery of St. Paul to give thanks. Her actions underscored the psychological advantage she and Ferdinand had achieved. More and more people gave her their support, believing the end was near and that Isabella would, indeed, become undisputed queen of Castile.

The war would drag on until 1479, but the overwhelming victory at Toro broke the Portuguese. In January 1477 Ferdinand and Isabella went to Toledo to begin the work of consolidating their victory. Again, they decided to separate to achieve their goals: Ferdinand went north, while Isabella traveled to Seville to deal with challenges to royal power in the south. That summer, Ferdinand joined her there, and on June 30, 1478, Castile rejoiced at the news of the birth of their son, Prince John, in Seville. He was the embodiment of their dreams, for he was recognized immediately as the true heir to the crowns of both Castile and Aragon. To celebrate, Isabella even allowed a bullfight, a tradition she abhorred, to be held.

In January 1479 King John II of Aragon died, and Ferdinand assumed the throne. In October, Alfonso surrendered, signing a treaty renouncing all rights for himself and Juana to the crown of Castile. He withdrew to Portugal, young Juana entered the convent of Santa Clara at Coimbra, and Isabella became undisputed queen of Castile. That same winter Isabella gave birth to her third child, the unhappy daughter destined for tragedy, Juana.

At last, 10 years after their secret wedding, the royal couple had their crowns, and they could turn their full attention to the positive, productive work of reorganizing the government and economy and consolidating royal power. There was much yet to be done before Ferdinand and Isabella could tackle the problem of the Moors in Granada.

4

A Country Comes Together

As one 15th-century writer put it, Ferdinand and Isabella hoped "to restore these kingdoms and rescue them from the tyrannical government to which they have for so long been subjected." They had spent the first 10 years of their marriage earning the right to fulfill this destiny, and by 1479 the time had come for them to pick up the pieces and put Castile back together.

They had already begun their work as early as 1476, when the victory at Toro had guaranteed them control of most of the country. In that year Ferdinand and Isabella formed a national police force. Based on the local vigilante groups called hermandades, the *Santa Hermandad* — "Holy Brotherhood" — patrolled the roads and countryside. The monarchs recruited common people in each town to serve in the force, thus forming an impartial network. If a criminal was being chased by the Santa Hermandad and the police in pursuit reached the edge of their jurisdiction, the chase would be picked up by the Santa Hermandad of the next town. In this way, the network proved extremely effective. The nobles, however, opposed the force because

Ferdinand and Isabella saw it as their mission to restore peace and order under the authority of the crown.
—MELVEENA MCKENDRICK
biographer

The cover of a 15th-century manual for knights shows a warrior declaring allegiance to his king. To consolidate their power in Castile, Ferdinand and Isabella first had to remove the bases of the nobles' power: their castles, private armies, and abundant wealth.

they found themselves being policed by their own servants, and they sought to undermine and break up the Santa Hermandad. Ferdinand and Isabella counteracted those efforts by creating a professional standing army of 2,000 well-trained soldiers to protect the network. Alfonso of Aragon, Ferdinand's half brother, was appointed head of the army.

In this way, law and order began to take hold all over Castile. But it was a cruel and swift justice that was applied, for the Santa Hermandad was given enormous latitude to deal with real or suspected criminals. When a suspect was caught, he was tried, sentenced, and punished then and there. The punishments were always severe and often barbaric. For a simple crime such as petty theft, a person was likely to have one of his hands or feet cut off; for anything more serious, instant execution was ordered. It was a reign of terror, but it worked. The crime rate began to drop, the numerous countryside hideouts for bandits were destroyed, and lawlessness began to disappear.

It had always been clear to the king and queen that for their idea of centralization of authority in the crown to work, the nobles, barons, and other grandees had to be stripped of their power. During the war Isabella had already undercut the orders of knights from which the nobles derived much of their unity. In 1476 Isabella had received news that the grand master of the Santiago knights had died. Santiago, along with Calatrava and Alcántara, had been targeted by Ferdinand and Isabella as aristocratic organizations that would have to be brought under the control of the crown. Isabella saw the opportunity and acted immediately. She had been told that the members of Santiago were meeting in the convent at Uclés, 200 miles away (Isabella was in Valladolid at the time), to choose a successor to the grand master. With a small, hastily assembled party, she traveled on horseback day and night for three days to reach Uclés. She burst in on the meeting, visibly shocking the electors, and proceeded to nominate Ferdinand as the new grand master of Santiago. To the order's members her intentions

Ferdinand and Isabella had to deal with a double problem— that of uniting two kingdoms that did not want to be united, and that of giving them a king and queen they did not want either.
—MAURICE ROWDON
British historian

A page from the 15th-century *Aureum opus* — the Golden Book — depicts a jousting helmet from Valencia. The monarchs' social reforms in Castile perhaps inspired the publication of the book, a compilation of traditional Aragonese laws dating to the 13th century.

could not have been clearer, but there was little they could do to prevent Isabella from getting her way. "Besides," Isabella is reported to have said, "such an important order of knights deserves no one less eminent than the king himself at its head." In one brilliant move, the shrewd queen had wrested this power away from the nobles. Ferdinand, of course, won the election handily and, in an equally brilliant political move, appointed his chief rival to act as head of the organization in his absence. By 1499 the royal couple would succeed in taking over all three orders of knighthood. They subsequently reformed the orders, funneling most of the revenues and resources into the royal treasury and making membership subject to appointment by the crown.

Even after the decisive victory at Toro, the monarchs still had to face pockets of resistance within Castile. The problem was particularly acute in the far north and in the southern provinces of Estremadura and Andalusia. In 1477 Ferdinand and Isabella set out to subdue the grandees in these areas. While Ferdinand went north to reduce the aristocracy there to subservience, Isabella used her great powers of persuasion to regain control of the towns of Trujillo and Cáceres in Estremadura. Then she continued her activity in Andalusia, where in a masterful diplomatic stroke she ended without bloodshed the long, bitter feud between Enrique de Guzmán, the powerful duke of Medina-Sidonia, and Rodrigo Ponce de León, marqués of Cádiz. Both noblemen turned over their fortresses to the queen.

In late 1479 Ferdinand and Isabella ordered the Cortes to meet them in Toledo to set up desperately needed reforms. The Toledo Cortes, which began its sessions in early 1480, was a crucial one for the development of Spain. Working together with the legislators, the monarchs first attacked the power

The Golden Book contained a history of Aragon, including the story of King James the Conqueror, who won renown during the Reconquest. The work may have been an attempt to raise in Aragon the kind of national identity Ferdinand and Isabella were fostering in Castile.

bases of the aristocracy. They ordered that the castles and other fortresses of the grandees be razed. What followed was, perhaps, one of the saddest times in the history of Castile. Castile means country of castles; demolishing them amounted to destroying the country's history. Thousands of these stone architectural marvels were leveled; in the northwestern region of Galicia alone, almost 50 castles were destroyed. Furthermore, the king and queen made it illegal for anyone to erect fortresses without royal permission. Without such fortifications, military activity on the part of the nobles became impossible.

Ferdinand and Isabella next attacked the old privileges of the noblemen. Dueling, nothing more than a thinly disguised license for killing an opponent, was made a treasonable offense punishable by death. The monarchs forced the nobles to swear to "keep the peace among themselves," making them accountable directly to the throne for any act of aggression. Suddenly, the grandees were no longer above the law. Many of their traditional ceremonies were abolished, and the appointment of people to various court offices or functions came to be based not on wealth or position but on merit. Naturally, the grandees were indignant over their sudden misfortune. Several of them banded together and wrote letters of vigorous protest to the king and queen. But these letters were answered with such a stern reprimand that the aristocrats immediately retreated from their positions. It was clear that the throne had acquired the power to enforce its wishes; the grandees had no choice but to acquiesce to the new order.

Ferdinand and Isabella attacked the principal source of the nobles' power: money. They decreed that each noble was to return to the crown half of all the revenues he had collected or taken from the country or from the throne over the previous 16 years. The nobles were outraged but remained powerless to oppose such a demand, for their armies had been dispersed and their fortresses largely destroyed.

> *The monarchs were most careful to place men of prudence and ability to serve, even though such were of the middling sort rather than the noblest houses.*
> —GALINDEZ DE CARBEJAL
> adviser to Ferdinand and Isabella, on the royal effort to control the nobles' power

This portion of the town walls of Ávila indicates the strong defensible positions the nobles relied on to maintain their power. As a check on the nobles' power Ferdinand and Isabella destroyed thousands of fortified castles throughout Castile.

To ensure the success of this program, Isabella appointed her confessor, Hernando de Talavera, head of the operation. He was so successful that the royal treasury received about 30 million *maravedís* (the standard currency), an extraordinary amount of money in 1480. Castile was now financially sound, and by the middle of the decade the independent nobility had been rendered powerless.

As village officials took on more and more new administrative duties, many towns began to acquire powers the old local aristocracy had held. The Cortes came to be dominated by representatives from the villages. Ferdinand and Isabella, wary of any group or assembly that could possibly challenge the authority of the throne, devised a means to maintain royal control among the towns. They created a new set of officials known as *corregidores* and appointed one as the head of each town. Each corregidor was given both administrative and judicial powers over his village, and each was responsible directly to the crown. This meant that the king and queen had a combination mayor/spy in each town. Every correg-idor had to report on the affairs of his community. If the king or queen felt something was wrong, the corregidor was told to correct it. If he failed, he was replaced.

The monarchs ordered a codification of the laws in an effort to regularize the legal system through-out the country. Isabella appointed a renowned ju-rist, Alfonso Díaz de Montalvo, to consolidate the laws. His compilation, the *Ordenanzas Reales* (Royal Ordinances) served as the basis for modern Spanish jurisprudence. The royal legal reforms also included regular jail inspections and the establish-ment of public funds for the defense of the poor.

Some of the most far-reaching reforms Ferdinand and Isabella carried out were economic. To put the national currency once more on a solid foundation, they drastically reduced the number of mints and forbade the private minting of coins. They restruc-tured the trade laws, realizing that commerce was an important source of income that needed to re-main under royal control. They standardized import and export tariffs, abolishing taxes altogether on goods traded between Aragon and Castile. They set up royal licensing of commercial ventures and es-tablished customs controls, which would prove of immense value to the crown when the wealth from the New World began to flow in. As more and more people came to have confidence in the financial structure of the country, both internal and external trade began to flourish.

As the royal reforms brought the monarchs their desired aims of creating a centralized authority, a stable economy, and a responsible administrative structure, Isabella turned her attention to reform-ing the Spanish church. Earlier, before the war with Portugal had broken out, the monarchs had begun a campaign of reform by threatening a public in-vestigation of the abuses and corruption within the Church. Pope Sixtus IV, faced with the possibility of having the entire Spanish church overthrown, acquiesced to the demands of the king and queen and allowed the crown to regain much of the juris-

To assert royal control over the economy and thus regu-late the nobles' incomes, Ferdinand and Isabella insti-tuted a number of economic reforms. Coins such as this *excelente* replaced the de-based money issued by Henry IV.

diction it had once had over official appointments. Ferdinand and Isabella replaced many of the inferior ecclesiastics with far more worthy people: Scholars, historians, and scientists, all deeply devout and all men of integrity, were given important stations. Now the devout queen wanted to be certain her state rested on a solid moral foundation, with a unified, spiritually sound church, before undertaking the crusade against the Moors. In 1478 Ferdinand and Isabella requested permission from Pope Sixtus to establish an inquisition — a council to root out heretics — and by 1480 the first inquisitors were appointed in Seville. Inquisitions were not new; such bodies had existed in Europe for centuries. In Spain, however, the inquisition would become notorious.

Within 10 years most of the royal reforms were instituted and operating. It is indicative of the single-minded vision of Ferdinand and Isabella that such a drastic change took place in a relatively short period of time. The monarchs continued to receive reports on all aspects of their realm and did not hesitate to reduce in power or abolish any office that had outlived its purpose. Toward the end of the 1480s, Ferdinand and Isabella began to dismantle the Santa Hermandad. The police network had done its job; crime was drastically reduced, and travelers no longer needed to worry about brigands. Furthermore, the justice that the Santa Hermandad administered seemed too severe for the new climate in the country. Accordingly, the monarchs sharply curtailed the force's autonomy. Sentences were reduced, and convicted criminals were allowed to appeal. Perhaps the royal couple came to feel that the kind of barbarism shown by the Santa Hermandad, if left unchecked, could generate a backlash against the crown. Justice, after all, should have a sense of fairness, and the Santa Hermandad was never known for its evenhandedness. Whatever their reasons, within a short time, Ferdinand and Isabella reduced the Santa Hermandad to the status of a small-town police force.

Twenty years had passed since the royal wedding

The Santa Hermandad came to exercise a reign of terror over the Castilian countryside. It was dealing with a savage society, and its methods were correspondingly savage.
—MELVEENA MCKENDRICK
biographer

Pope Sixtus IV was compelled to return to the Spanish monarchs control over ecclesiastical appointments in Spain. Ferdinand and Isabella replaced corrupt clergymen with men of true faith and ability.

in Valladolid. Those years had seen Isabella fight, maneuver, and politicize her way into the sovereignty of Castile. She had fought and won a major war, then stripped all possible opponents of their power. Ferdinand had been at her side almost constantly, due in part to the fact that he had been able to appoint a viceroy to govern his own kingdom of Aragon, which overall had been less troubled than Castile. Together, Ferdinand and Isabella had taken many shattered fragments and welded them together into a strong country. With the unification of Aragon and Castile assured by virtue of their young son, Prince John, the monarchs could turn their attention to the goal of reclaiming the last portion of Spain still under foreign rule. It was time for them to drive the Moors out of the country. They would have to conquer Granada.

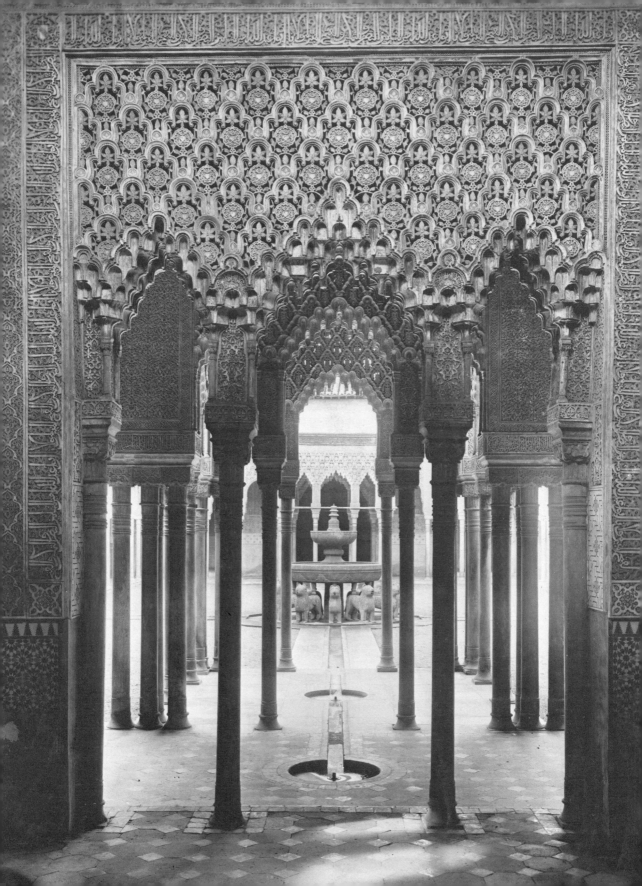

5

The Fall of Granada

Ever since she was a child, Isabella had been driven by two profound desires. The first was to be as deeply devout a Catholic as ever lived. The second was to unify Spain. Throughout her life she had interwoven these two aims, so that unification of Spain had become as much a religious crusade as it was an act of nationalism. The reconquest of Granada, then, was viewed by the queen as the most important goal of her life.

When the Moors had been driven south, they had regrouped in the small southern country of Granada, where they had been firmly entrenched for 250 years. Isabella's half brother, Henry IV of Castile, had sent armies to invade the country on at least six different occasions between 1455 and 1459. None had been successful.

Granada, with a population of perhaps 3 million in 1480, had long been a bustling commercial and artistic center in the Moorish empire, famous for its exquisite, intricate metalwork. Although by the 15th century it was long past the glory days of the Muslim empire, the small country still contained several important cities and was peppered with more than 100 strong fortresses. In the capital city of Granada were found the two lavish, exotic palaces for which the city was known — the Albaicín and the

This majestic fountain lies in the Court of the Lions within the Alhambra, the magnificent palace that housed the Moorish rulers of Granada. After establishing control in Castile Ferdinand and Isabella conducted the greatest struggle of their reign to free southern Spain from Moorish domination.

The Alhambra sits atop a hill overlooking Granada, the capital city of the kingdom of Granada. The Moors held a nearly impenetrable domain protected by the Sierra Nevadas to the north and open to the Mediterranean in the south.

Alhambra. With its natural fortifications, it was an easy country to defend. Ringed by rugged mountains to the north, west, and east, Granada enjoyed a difficult, rocky terrain as a formidable line of defense. Its coastline to the south gave the Moors easy access to North Africa and the Mediterranean Sea, and the Moors controlled two important ports — Málaga and Almería — through which they could receive supplies and reinforcements.

Their presence on Spanish soil was a constant source of dismay and consternation to the king and queen as well as to Christian Europe. Many countries were concerned that Granada would offer a friendly port not only to the Moors of North Africa, who could, conceivably, begin to advance once again, but also to the Muslim Ottoman Turks. The Turks had captured Constantinople in 1453 and were pushing north toward central Europe.

One great advantage the Spanish had was that Granada was beset by internal rivalries. Since 1466 the king of the Moors had been Mulay Hassan. Many believed that he did, indeed, harbor the ambition to reconquer all of Spain. But by 1480 Mulay Hassan was an old man, and he faced two rivals: his brother, who was known as El Zagal ("the Valiant"), and one of his sons, Abu Abd Allah Muhammad, whom the Spaniards called Boabdil. Still, an uneasy truce between Hassan and Castile, arranged when the Moors had been driven south, remained in place. The agreement provided that Granada would pay a yearly fee to Castile in return for which the two countries would not interfere with each other.

In 1478, however, Granada refused to pay. Mulay Hassan appeared to be taking advantage of the turmoil over the succession in Castile; the final peace with Portugal had not yet been concluded, and Ferdinand and Isabella were busy with their internal reforms. When Ferdinand and Isabella sent a messenger to Hassan demanding the annual tribute, the Moor replied, in a message tantamount to a declaration of war, "The mints of Granada no longer coin gold, but steel." Ferdinand and Isabella were in no position to seek retribution; they did not have the resources to wage another war.

In October 1481 the marqués of Cádiz attacked a Moorish outpost. In December, Mulay Hassan took his revenge by sacking Zahara, a Christian town on the western border of Granada that was also a gateway into Andalusia. The Moors massacred all the men in the town, and the women and children were bound into slavery. Ferdinand and Isabella, spending the Christmas holidays at Medina del Campo, were much too far away to offer aid, but orders flew south to build up the border fortresses. By this time, of course, Isabella had won her crown, and the war with Portugal had ended. Consequently, Ferdinand and Isabella could now turn the full force of their army against the Moors.

On February 28, 1482, Cádiz and his men attacked Alhama, a town well into Granadan territory. In the dead of night, the small band scaled the walls of the fortress, overpowered the gatekeepers, and threw open the gates. The Alhamans fought back viciously, engaging the Castilians in a battle that

This ivory box shows the influence of Moorish art in Spain. For many years Granada had been an artistic center, known for its intricate metalwork, within the Moorish empire that extended across North Africa.

lasted until sunset. Finally, at dusk, the Castilians took control. They had killed about 1,000 Moors and captured thousands more.

Twenty-five miles away, Mulay Hassan received news of the defeat. He quickly assembled an army of 50,000 men to retake Alhama. But Ferdinand was riding down from the north with reinforcements, and Isabella, raising both money and supplies, was also on her way; she would rendezvous with Ferdinand at Córdoba, a town safely in Andalusia yet within striking distance of Christian-held Alhama. Once again, Isabella found herself riding squarely into the face of danger despite the fact that she was pregnant with her fourth child. "Glory is not to be won without danger," she told her advisers, and the Traveling Queen set up her court in Córdoba. (In June, after a difficult labor, Isabella would bear a daughter, María, and 35 hours later, María's twin sister was born dead.)

Hassan, afraid of being caught between Alhama and Ferdinand's army, retreated to the city of Granada, and Alhama remained in the hands of the Christians. Isabella took immediate action. She sanctified all the Arab mosques (places of worship) in the city; then they were reconsecrated as Catholic churches. The king concentrated on building, training, and drilling his army. Together, the two monarchs set about implementing their plans to conquer the rest of Granada.

Ferdinand's technique was ruthlessly simple. As the army advanced, it destroyed everything in its path. Crops were burned, towns and villages were leveled, and supplies were destroyed. The attackers made slow progress, mostly because of transportation difficulties. Trails had to be cut, bridges built, and often the soldiers themselves had to help the mules and oxen pull the heavy loads, especially in the mountains. Ultimately, the army destroyed not only its enemies but also the countryside, for Ferdinand's "scorched earth" policy left the *vega*, the open plain that was Granada's farmland, charred and black. Ferdinand's policy was indeed destructive, but strategically important for the Spanish. By

destroying the Moors' food supply, Ferdinand tried to shorten the war.

The king also waged war from the sea by sending an armada to set up a blockade around Granada. Slowly, the campaign gained both momentum and support. Each Christian victory prompted more Spaniards to join the cause; the monarchs' crusade served as a powerful unifying force in the rest of the country.

Once again, Ferdinand and Isabella proved to be an almost unbeatable team, each being extraordinarily proficient at his or her specific duties. Ferdinand led the army; Isabella provided the funding, along with a humanitarian spirit rarely displayed by a monarch. At her own expense she created the Queen's Hospitals — a series of six huge tents set up at battle sites to provide the best possible medical attention for the sick and wounded. She also created primitive ambulances — 400 covered and armored

This building in Córdoba, in southern Spain, retains the original Moorish architecture of a mosque. As Ferdinand and Isabella captured Moorish towns in Granada, the queen ordered all the mosques consecrated and converted into churches.

wagons that transported the injured to the hospitals. As always, she remained highly visible, particularly in the hospitals, where she gave aid and comfort to the soldiers.

After the success at Alhama, though, the Spanish met with some embarrassing defeats. In spring 1482, the day after the birth of his daughter María, Ferdinand attempted to take Loja, 15 miles from Alhama, but was ignominiously repelled. In fact, the king was saved from capture only through a daring rescue by Cádiz. The following March an army led by Alonso de Cárdenas, grand master of Santiago, attempted a raid on the Axarquia, a fertile valley north of the strategically vital port of Málaga. El Zagal and his men fell upon the Castilians in a fierce ambush; the Spanish panicked and fled, becoming desperately lost in a deep ravine. When daylight broke, they found themselves in a valley, where the confused, bumbling soldiers surrendered to a lesser number of Moors. Some who had tried to escape on foot were captured by Moorish women working in the fields. Others made it back through the mountains. The final losses were severe: 800 Spaniards were killed and another 2,000 captured.

Fortunately for the Spanish, however, civil strife

After suffering some initial defeats the Spanish monarchs decided to upgrade their armies. From European rulers Isabella received weapons such as this French cannon. Heavy cannon was the only weapon capable of blasting through the thick fortress walls.

broke out in Granada. Mulay Hassan's sons rebelled, and Boabdil, determined not to be outdone by El Zagal, in April organized an army of 10,000 to march against the Andalusian town of Lucena, southeast of Córdoba. Boabdil proved an incompetent leader, and the attack was a disaster; he himself was captured by an ordinary Castilian foot soldier.

The crafty Ferdinand, seeing the divisiveness among the Moors, moved swiftly to use Boabdil to his advantage. The Moor was given his freedom after turning over a sum of money and Christian captives and was told he would be recognized ruler of any towns he could hold, but he first had to control Granada, the capital, where Mulay Hassan was now entrenched. Boabdil sneaked into Granada to stir up a civil war against his father.

As the internal conflict raged on in Granada, Ferdinand and Isabella rethought their strategy. Isabella sent representatives to Italy, Germany, France, and other European countries sympathetic to her cause, asking for specialists and supplies. She acquired primitive lombards — large, clumsy cannons capable of shooting iron and marble balls weighing up to 165 pounds apiece. They were unwieldy and sometimes unreliable, but when they worked, they allowed Ferdinand to blast through the thick stone walls of the Moorish fortresses. When provided in addition with lighter, more easily transported cannons, the Spanish army had 2,000 pieces of artillery at its command. Ferdinand and Isabella spent most of 1484 refitting, arming, and training the army for the reconquest. By spring 1485 the king was ready to resume the war; during this year Isabella had her last child, Catherine.

In May 1485, after a 10-day siege, Ferdinand captured Ronda, a fortress in western Granada that had been considered impregnable. Its fall thoroughly dismayed the Moors, and 94 of the towns in western Granada gave themselves up to the Spanish. That same month, Ferdinand took Loja, the scene of his earlier failure, and once again captured the hapless Boabdil, who had fled the capital after losing to his

In the minds of Spaniards down to the present day, no event has been more closely associated with Ferdinand and Isabella than the conquest of Granada.
—MELVEENA MCKENDRICK
biographer

This royal decree secures the appointment of a justice minister in a Moorish town captured in 1480. Ferdinand and Isabella were usually lenient toward the Moors, but in 1487 they condemned the entire population of Málaga to slavery as an example to the remaining opposition.

father. Boabdil was released to stir up more trouble among the Moors. After the battle at Loja the Spanish army had grown to 70,000 in a groundswell of support for Ferdinand and Isabella's crusade. The king now turned his sights on Málaga.

The capture of Málaga was of critical importance to Ferdinand and Isabella because it remained the only significant seaport the Moors were able to keep open. It was also a natural fortress, ringed on the north by tough, craggy mountains and on the south by the sea. The siege began in spring 1487. Ferdinand launched an armada to blockade the port from the sea. With his heavy artillery firing continuously at the stone walls, the king was able to take the Málagan suburbs only with difficulty. Inside the besieged city itself, the Moorish commander executed any troops who contemplated surrender — he was determined to hold out.

Ferdinand had Francisco Ramírez, an army engineer from Madrid, design and build a new kind of assault vehicle — huge wooden towers on rollers that were higher than the walls of Málaga. The vehicles, loaded with soldiers, were rolled right up to the walls of the city; the soldiers inside simply dropped down over the battlements onto their enemies. Unfortunately, not enough soldiers could drop down at once. When they landed, they were hopelessly outnumbered. Ferdinand's men were killed and his towers destroyed.

Ferdinand's attack stalled, and the frustrated king sent for Isabella. She encouraged both her husband and the troops, and the Spanish army renewed the assault. Ferdinand had only to wait, for his combined land and sea assault had cut off all of the Moors' supply routes. By August the starving Málagans, reduced to eating their cats and dogs, had had enough and offered to surrender to Ferdinand on his usual terms.

Ferdinand and Isabella had always been unusually generous to captured cities. Everyone was given the choice of leaving the country with their personal belongings or of becoming Spanish citizens while retaining the right to their own religion and cus-

> *The desire which we have to serve God and our zeal for the holy Catholic faith has induced us to set aside our own interests and ignore the continual hardships and dangers to which this cause commits us.*
> —FERDINAND AND ISABELLA statement to Pope Sixtus IV, on Granada

toms. But when Málaga offered to surrender on these terms, Ferdinand refused, insisting on nothing less than unconditional surrender. The Málagans threatened to kill the Christians in the city if their terms were not met. Enraged, Ferdinand swore he would massacre the Málagans if they hurt any of the captive Christians. The Málagans, defeated, starving, and fearful that Ferdinand would prove true to his threat, surrendered without conditions.

On August 18, 1487, Ferdinand and Isabella entered Málaga as its conquerors. They condemned the entire population to slavery: One-third would be exchanged for Christian prisoners held in North Africa, another third would be indentured (made servants) to the throne, and the final third would be given over to those who supported the long war. Ferdinand offered the captives a chance to buy their freedom, but few could afford the sum. By imposing the harsh sentence of slavery upon the entire population, Ferdinand and Isabella hoped to frighten the Moors in the rest of the country into surrendering quickly.

The monarchs held the west of Granada. El Zagal — who now claimed the kingship because Mulay Hassan had died — had firm control over most of eastern Granada. Boabdil had returned to the Alhambra in the capital, Granada. Neither Ferdinand nor Isabella had any intention of allowing Boabdil to remain ruler of the city, but they knew a direct attack there was destined to fail. The monarchs decided to reduce the east and then attempt to take the great city in the center. In May 1489 Ferdinand, at the head of a 100,000-strong army, led the assault on Baza, a major city in the northeast held by El Zagal's brother-in-law, Cid Hiaya.

It was a very difficult campaign for the Castilian army. Cid Hiaya, an extremely capable leader, conducted damaging, demoralizing raids on the Spanish camp. Funds were running low, and Isabella, who had relocated her headquarters to Jaén, had to borrow money against her jewels to continue financing the venture. The autumn brought an unusual amount of rainfall, creating severe flooding

The war was not all stark and grim. It was carried on with the pomp and grandeur thought appropriate to a religious crusade. The nobles set up camp in silken tents, and richly liveried servants offered them food on gold and silver plates.
—MELVEENA MCKENDRICK
biographer, on the
conquest of Granada

that virtually washed away the camp. Again, it was the queen who turned the tide; in November she made another personal appearance. "Her presence filled us with joy and reanimated our spirits," recalled an observer. The queen seemed to give new life to the troops and restore their resolve. As if to confirm the superstition that Isabella's presence worked magic, three days later Baza suddenly, inexplicably, offered to surrender. (It has been suggested that the Moors were bribed to give up.)

In this case, Ferdinand offered the most generous conditions. His only provision was that the mayor of Baza help convince El Zagal to surrender the rest of the territories he controlled. When confronted with the accomplished fact, El Zagal had little choice. "What Allah wills, He brings to pass in his own way," he declared. Baza surrendered on December 4, and Ferdinand and Isabella took the keys to Almería just before Christmas. The east was theirs, and Granada, the heart of the country, was left isolated, its lifelines cut off.

The campaign to take Granada began the following spring. Boabdil had reneged on his agreement with Ferdinand and declared that he would continue the struggle to defend what was left of Moorish territory. He insolently launched several raids into nearby Christian-occupied territory. The king and

Boabdil, last king of the Moors, surrenders the capital city of Granada to Ferdinand and Isabella in January 1492. The citizens of Granada had been reduced to starvation by Ferdinand's long siege of the city.

69

Las Alpujarras was the small mountain kingdom to which Boabdil was exiled in 1492. Although nominal ruler, Boabdil was to remain under Spanish royal jurisdiction. With his departure, Ferdinand and Isabella controlled all of Granada.

queen built a huge encampment in plain sight of the city and laid waste to the vega. They cut off the city's supply lines and prepared to wait out the siege. Then near tragedy struck.

One evening, as Isabella slept, one of her servants moved a lighted candle away from her face so the flickering light would not disturb her sleep. But the candle was placed too close to the tent fabric, and suddenly the silk caught fire. The flames spread so rapidly that fighting the fire was pointless. The camp became a virtual inferno and quickly burned to the ground. Miraculously, no one was injured, and the next day the army began to rebuild. This time, however, they erected not tents of silk but an entire city. Buildings, churches, and roads were constructed — all within 90 days. The soldiers wanted to name the new city after Isabella, but she declined, asking instead that the shining white city constructed in the form of a cross be named Santa Fé—the City of Holy Faith.

By mid-1491 the citizens in Granada were desperate. When they saw an entire city rise from ashes in less than three months, they began to lose hope. They sought ways to meet the Castilian army on more even terms. For instance, they suggested that the soldiers fight one at a time in individual challenges. Of course, the Castilians refused; they had the advantage and intended to keep it.

In October 1491, realizing he was beaten and afraid of his enemies within the city, Boabdil began secret negotiations with representatives of Ferdinand and Isabella. The king and queen sent Hernando de Zafra, the royal secretary, and Gonzalo de Córdoba, an army officer who spoke Arabic, to negotiate. Ferdinand's terms were relatively liberal: In exchange for total surrender, the Moors would be given their religious freedom and be allowed to administer their own laws, observe their own traditions of customs and dress, and keep their personal property. They would even be granted a three-year waiting period before they were to pay any taxes. Boabdil would be given the small kingdom of neighboring Las Alpujarras in the southern mountains, but he would remain under Spanish jurisdiction. The terms were designed for maximum political impact; Ferdinand knew he needed to evoke a sense of gratitude from the Moors in order to make more secure his rather tenuous position as their ruler.

On January 2, 1492, Boabdil departed from the Alhambra. When he reached Ferdinand and Isabella, he tried to kiss the king's hand, but Ferdinand refused, thinking it too demeaning. Boabdil kissed the king's sleeve instead, then rode off toward Las Alpujarras and obscurity. Shortly thereafter, a specially selected band of Castilian soldiers rode into Granada, entered the Alhambra, and raised a huge silver cross above it. Moments later the royal flag was raised alongside it. Shouts of joy rang out from everywhere as Isabella was proclaimed queen of Granada. As the full impact of their accomplishment hit them, Ferdinand and Isabella knelt on the ground to give silent thanks. In a giant wave the entire army followed them, linked with the king and queen in a moment too precious for speeches. After almost 800 years, Spain was united and free.

6

In the Name of God

The year 1492 was indeed a momentous one for Spain. Ferdinand and Isabella had liberated Spain from the Moors. Congratulations poured in from European monarchs grateful for any victory against the Muslims, who in the form of the Ottoman Turks were threatening the east and south. Isabella sent Columbus on his voyage west. Except for an attack on Ferdinand at the end of the year by a madman who cut a severe gash in his neck, the monarchs could be pleased with the year's events. For some Spaniards, however, 1492 held only misery.

Jews had lived in Spain for hundreds of years. In Christian Visigothic Spain the Jews were persecuted. When the Moors subdued the Visigoths in the 8th century, the Jews were left in peace. But in the 12th century, Muslim fanatics among the Moors rekindled the old flames of oppression, and many Jews fled to the Christian communities of the north.

During the long years of the Reconquest, Christians, Jews, and *mudéjares* — those Moors living under Christians in liberated areas — all lived and worked together in relative peace. As one historian described the period: "In the commercial sphere no visible barriers separated Jewish, Christian, and

> *The religious orthodoxy smothered the humanity. In Spain, it smothered the beginnings of a great civilization.*
> —MAURICE ROWDON
> British historian

This 19th-century painting depicts a typical medieval *auto-da-fe*, the ritual punishment and burning at the stake of convicted heretics. Ferdinand and Isabella established the Spanish Inquisition in 1478 to realize their vision of a unified, homogeneous society.

Saracen [Moorish] merchants. . . . Christian contractors built Jewish houses and Jewish craftsmen worked for Christian employers. Jewish advocates [lawyers] represented Gentile clients in the secular courts. Jewish brokers acted as intermediaries between Christian and Moorish principals. As a by-product, such continuous daily contact inevitably fostered tolerance and friendly relationships."

Still, barriers between Christians and Jews remained. The Jews had achieved considerable status as doctors, lawyers, bankers, and treasury officials, and were well represented in most professional occupations. Resentment over this perceived inequity expressed itself as religious hatred. Anti-Semitism

Jewish communities existed in Spain prior to the rule of the Visigoths. In this 15th-century Catalan painting, Jesus preaches in a temple modeled on contemporary Spanish synagogues.

A 15th-century Hebrew Bible from Spain. The persecution of Jews in medieval Spain led many of them to convert to Christianity. These *conversos* were suspected of adopting the trappings but not the substance of their new faith.

arose, partly from old legend, partly from envy, fear, and greed. The Christians found many reasons for hatred; in their eyes, doctors were murderers, treasury officials were tax collectors, bankers were unscrupulous moneylenders, and the Jews in general had chosen professions to make easy money while escaping the rigors of "honest" hard labor. What was more, most of Europe held to the popular belief that Jews stole Christian children and sacrificed them in some mysterious religious ritual. (Surprisingly, the church did not address this issue until the 18th century, when an official investigation was held to lay to rest forever this absurd belief.)

In 1371 the Castilian Cortes had decreed that all Jews were to wear a round yellow patch over their hearts, a law that signaled the beginning of overt anti-Semitism among the population. In 1391 the Jewish sections of Toledo, Valencia, Barcelona, Seville, and other cities were destroyed; in June of that year, more than 4,000 Jews were killed in Seville. Many Jews became frightened and converted to Christianity. But these *marranos*, as they were called, fared even worse, because they were not trusted. In 1412 a law was passed depriving both Jews and Moors of "the right to hold office, to bear arms, to hire Christians to work for them, or to follow the trades of carpenter, tailor, butcher, or grocer." Jews were not allowed to move from one home to another or to eat, drink, bathe, or talk to Christians. They had to wear rough clothing with the yellow patch and had to keep their hair and beards long. This law alone led thousands of Jews to convert. (Moors also converted to Christianity; they were called *moriscos*; both Moors and Jews may be referred to as *conversos*, or "converts.") Soon, despite the sentiment against them, the conversos began to intermarry with Christians, and many converso families rose to power. Eventually, they were responsible for providing four of Isabella's own bishops, three royal secretaries, one of the queen's own confessors — Archbishop Hernando de Talavera of Granada — and the grand masters of Santiago and Calatrava. Even Ferdinand was reported to have some Jewish blood.

The old Spanish aristocracy became alarmed. They believed that they alone had "pure" blood and true faith and felt threatened by the assimilation of the conversos. They began calling themselves Old Christians to distinguish themselves from conversos. Beginning in 1449, with a decree in Toledo, the Old Christians were instrumental in gaining the passage of laws similar to the one of 1412 in virtually every city; the new strictures pertained to both Jews and conversos and forbade them from holding public office or testifying against an Old Christian.

Some prominent individuals resisted such bigotry. Archbishop Carrillo, the man who had married Ferdinand and Isabella, wrote, "Divisions bring great scandals and schism and divide the seamless garment of Christ, who, as the Good Shepherd, commanded us to love one another in unity and

> *Intolerance was in the air, and Ferdinand and Isabella were swept up in this by virtue of their religious zeal.*
> —MAURICE ROWDON
> British historian

obedience to Holy Mother Church." But he was part of only a small minority and despite his rank and position could do little against the forces of prejudice and selfish interests.

Isabella herself ranked high on the list of the culpable. She believed without question the teachings of the church and was convinced that spiritual and even racial unity was necessary for a strong Spain. One of her early confessors, Tomás de Torquemada, told her, "Should you ever come to the throne, you will undertake the sacred mission of stamping out heresy." When she lived in Seville in 1477–78, she was subjected to constant anticonverso propaganda from Alfonso de Hojeda, prior of the Dominican Monastery at St. Paul. For 15 months, the fanatical priest bombarded Isabella and others with his violent anticonverso sermons. In 1478, under pressure from high church officials, Ferdinand and Isabella requested and received from Pope Sixtus IV permission to conduct "an inquisition to stamp out heresy and enforce religious orthodoxy." However, the church would not be in control; the government of Ferdinand and Isabella would run the Spanish

The passionate Cardinal Tomás de Torquemada raises a crucifix before Ferdinand and Isabella. In 1483 Torquemada was appointed first inquisitor general of the Spanish Inquisition.

Inquisition. Isabella, who always preferred gentle persuasion to direct pressure and force, was reluctant to start, and although the Holy Office was established in Spain, it was not until 1480 that the queen appointed the first inquisitors. In 1483 Torquemada was made inquisitor general (director of the holy tribunal) by Pope Sixtus; he reorganized the council and instituted standard questioning procedures. The use of torture was an accepted means of extracting confessions, and Torquemada established rules for exactly what kinds of torture could be used and in what manner. He held control over the appointment of inquisitors, subject, of course, to the queen's approval. Because of his high position Torquemada was also appointed to the royal council, so Isabella and Ferdinand were kept

Seville Cathedral dominates the city where the Spanish Inquisition began. The tribunal originally tried only conversos who were believed to have lapsed into their original faith.

aware of the actions of the Inquisition. It dealt only with those who were baptized conversos, for only they could be guilty of heresy. Practicing Jews and Moors were thus originally exempted, but eventually the Inquisition was widened to include them in order to achieve absolute "unity" of race and religion. The Spanish Inquisition started in Seville and immediately established an ominous precedent of anonymous accusation. "All citizens are to report to the authorities anyone and everyone they suspect of heresy," it was declared. Within a few months the authorities were inundated with accusations, and there were so many suspects in jail that a fortress outside Seville was needed to house the prisoners. Some citizens were deeply disturbed by the practice of anonymous accusation, claiming that it could be (and most certainly was) used by people simply to gain revenge or dispose of anyone for almost any reason. Simply being accused was grounds for arrest, and the accused was often left to languish in jail for months on end, awaiting a trial, not knowing who his accuser was or of what he was accused. The inquisitors defended this policy, claiming it to be the only way in which "a poor man could accuse a rich one, without fear of reprisal." Any activity that could be construed as "Jewish behavior," which

A meeting of the Grand Council of the Inquisition. The practice of anonymous accusation meant that victims often were unaware of the reason for their arrest and were unable to confront their accusers.

This 16th-century engraving depicts some of the tortures used to extract confessions from heretics. The Spanish Inquisition was not a unique phenomenon; the Catholic church had sanctioned such bodies for centuries to punish heretics.

would indicate that the converso had not fully embraced Christianity, was grounds for an accusation of heresy. Under the increasing cloud of paranoia even the Old Christians began to fear; simply donning clean clothes on the Sabbath could be declared "Jewish behavior." Four thousand families fled Andalusia, but because harboring refugees was considered heresy, few of them succeeded. A group of conversos in Seville, led by Diego de Susán, one of the city's wealthiest and most respected citizens, decided to fight the Inquisition. He was joined by others from the city and surrounding countryside; together, it has been said, they might have put a stop to the Inquisition before it got out of hand. But Susán was betrayed by his own daughter, Susanna, who had an Old Christian lover. Afraid that if fighting erupted, her lover might be hurt, she turned in her father. Susán and his compatriots were arrested.

Six people, including Susán, were convicted by the church of the ultimate crime of heresy; they were handed over to the city officials. On February 6, 1481, the first *auto-da-fé* ("act of faith") was held. In a parade through the streets of the city, condemned heretics were publicly displayed before their execution. According to its own tenets, the church was forbidden to take life and so did not carry out the sentences it imposed; rather, it "relaxed to the secular arm" (gave over to the civil authorities) those to be executed. During the public procession the condemned were forced to wear *sanbenitos*, penitential garments. The "reconciled prisoners" — those not sentenced to death — wore yellow sanbenitos with diagonal crosses. Those condemned to death wore black sanbenitos with paintings of demons and hellfire on them. The city officials then completed the auto-da-fé by burning the convicted heretics at the stake. After the sentence was carried out, the sanbenito was hung in the prisoner's parish church to serve as a reminder. Often, after the years had turned the garments to dust, they were replaced with new ones to keep reminding everyone of the condemned person's heresy. Not all the convicted were condemned to death; lesser sentences included imprisonment, exile, confiscation of possessions, scourging, or confinement as a galley slave. A few days after the first auto-da-fé, Diego de Susán was burned at the stake.

Convicted heretics were required to wear penitential cloaks, called *sanbenitos*, during a public procession. Those sentenced to death wore sanbenitos bearing demons and hellfire.

By 1488, in Seville alone, about 700 people had been burned to death and more than 5,000 sentenced. It is estimated that during Isabella's reign, 2,000 people lost their lives at the hands of the Inquisition. Torquemada, who retained control of the holy tribunal until his death in 1498, was responsible for most of the executions. Paranoia about heretics permeated society as tribunals sprang up all over Spain. By 1486 the Inquisition had even been established throughout Ferdinand's kingdom of Aragon, traditionally more tolerant than Castile.

With the conversos under control, the government turned its attention to non-Christians. The remaining practicing Jews were confined to the

Ferdinand and Isabella hold an audience with a deputation of Jews. On March 30, 1492, the monarchs announced that all the Jews in Spain had to convert to Catholicism or leave the country. Their loss was a serious blow to the economy.

ghettos, and the yellow patch law was enforced. On March 30, 1492, Ferdinand and Isabella announced the notorious edict that forced all Jews either to convert or leave Spain. Approximately 150,000 Jews fled, selling all their worldly goods to get money for transportation. They streamed onto overcrowded ships, many of which were unseaworthy. Most of those that did not sink turned around and returned to Spain, where their passengers were forcibly converted. A few reached the coast of North Africa, only to be captured by the Moors. A rabbi described the general horror thus: "The Turks [Moors] killed to take out the gold which [the refugees] had swallowed to hide it; some of them hunger and the plague consumed and some of them were cast naked by the captains on the isles of the sea; and some of them were sold for men-servants or maid-servants in Genoa and its villages and some of them were cast into the sea."

The forced conversions of the Jews who remained

created a whole new society of conversos, which only served to intensify the problem the Inquisition was meant to solve. Moreover, heresy was believed to be hereditary; once a heretic was uncovered, his whole family was condemned; once convicted, the sentence was in force for years, sometimes for generations.

Isabella and Ferdinand expelled the Jews from Spain because they believed that without them Spain could achieve social stability and religious purity. The Moors, meanwhile, had been exempted from the Inquisition by Ferdinand, who ordered that they be "left in peace." But under the tyrannical leadership of Torquemada and Francisco Jiménez de Cisneros, who became archbishop of Toledo in 1495, it became clear that the Moors, too, would soon be persecuted.

In 1499 Archbishop Francisco Jiménez de Cisneros of Toledo led the campaign to forcibly convert the Muslim Moors. He destroyed centuries of scholarship when he had the Arabic libraries stripped and their books burned.

With the establishment of the Inquisition, religious fear permeated Spanish society. This early 16th-century bookbinding shows people burning in purgatorial fires.

This 15th-century candlestick holder depicts both biblical scenes and popular saints. In 1495 Isabella joined forces with Archbishop Cisneros to purge the Spanish church of corrupt, wealthy clergy.

After the conquest of Granada, of course, the number of Moors under Christian rule had greatly increased. Archbishop Talavera tried to prevent forcible conversion by first preaching to the Muslims. He had even learned Arabic in hopes of communicating directly with them. But religious conversion did not necessarily mean cultural assimilation; the fact remained that the Moors were seen as an "alien" element in Spain. In 1499 Cisneros began a concentrated campaign of forcible conversion. In December 1499 he converted 3,000 Moors; within the following few months 50,000 Moors became moriscos. But conversion alone did not satisfy Cisneros; he decided to "destroy the source of Muslim teaching" and ordered that all Arab books be confiscated. The libraries of Granada were stripped and a huge bonfire set; within hours, virtually all Arabic scholarship in Spain was destroyed. Into the conflagration went not only religious books, such as the Koran (the holy book of Islam), but thousands of magnificent secular works of literature and science. The Moors rose up in revolt, and only the influence of Talavera, joined by a number of well-respected city officials, was able to restore calm to the city.

Ferdinand was livid. The Inquisition was not primarily his concern, but the damage it did could be. He did not want another war with the Moors on his hands. Ferdinand vented his anger on the queen: "So we are like to pay dear for your archbishop, whose rashness has lost us in a few hours what we have been years in acquiring." Isabella was horrified and summoned Cisneros for an explanation. "We have acted in the right," the archbishop told her, "and for the true religion." So convincing was he that in February 1502 the queen ordered a "convert or leave" law enacted against the Moors.

Some Moors converted, to the ultimate consternation of the Inquisition, which had to deal with even more conversos; some fled to North Africa; and some took to the hills of Las Alpujarras, where they tried to resist enforcement of the law. But they were no match for the Spanish troops and were quickly subdued and killed.

This embroidered red velvet chasuble — a garment worn by a priest during mass — indicates the wealth the church commanded. Clerics who refused to renounce a worldly life-style were expelled from their offices or even excommunicated by Cisneros.

A painting of Santa Engracia by Bartolomeo Bermejo. Isabella's reform of the church largely prevented the 16th-century Protestant Reformation from taking hold in Spain, thus sparing the country great religious upheaval.

The work of the Inquisition was closely tied to Isabella's desire to reform the Spanish clergy, sunk in vice and corruption. After Cisneros became archbishop in 1495, he and the queen applied their considerable talents to this issue. Isabella traveled to convents, where she persuaded and cajoled the nuns to return to the simple life espoused by the early church. The archbishop, dressed in a plain brown robe and leading his mule, visited each monastery to catalog its land and wealth. He then exhorted the monks to give away what was not essential for their daily existence. Those clerics who clung to an opulent standard of living — including vast land holdings, servants, mistresses, and all the lesser trappings of wealth and power — faced harsher measures from the persistent Cisneros. If they were not suited to a monastic life, they were pensioned off. If they simply refused to reform, Cisneros had them thrown out of the order or even excommunicated. Each order was cleansed in turn —the Franciscans, Dominicans, the Carmelites.

When Isabella and Cisneros were through with the regulars (the monastic orders), they turned to the secular clergy. They applied the same pressures to rid the church of those who served only their own interests and neglected their spiritual duties. Isabella watched in content as her beloved church was nursed back to a degree of health.

By the beginning of the 16th century, the Spanish Inquisition had become an integral part of Spanish life. Together with Isabella's reform of the clergy the Inquisition was largely the reason the Protestant Reformation, which erupted in Germany in the early 1500s, would never take hold in Spain. The Inquisition insulated Spain from the religious and cultural changes going on all around it.

Isabella's view of progress was closely tied to her notion that everyone had to observe the one true religion, Catholicism, in order to unite Spain. Her vision of a strong, unified Spain was built around this idea. Her acceptance of the cruel methods employed by the Inquisition seems to pose an unsolvable contradiction. On the one hand, she was dedicated to the arts, the humanities, and the improvement of education. On the other, her rigid view of religion kept her country hopelessly isolated. The Spanish Inquisition actually destroyed many of Spain's sources of knowledge. The burning of Arabic books effectively erased hundreds of years of writing and scholarship; the eradication of the Jewish population removed scholars, writers, artists, musicians, and teachers. The people of Spain were relegated to a unidimensional society; there was no room to accept, or even listen to, new ideas. Far from improving the quality of life, the Spanish Inquisition became responsible for the murder of thousands of innocent people and the degradation of thousands more. The Inquisition was not abolished in Spain until 1834. The result of 350 years under its influence was a narrowing of the cultural fabric of Spanish society that ultimately rendered Spain conservative and backward while the rest of Europe advanced. Isabella's dream ultimately developed into a nightmare for Spain.

7
Of Politics and Power

The court of Ferdinand and Isabella was quite different from earlier Spanish courts. To be sure, there were the expected nobles and aspirants seeking political power, ladies-in-waiting attending the queen, religious leaders attempting to influence the court, and many others simply seeking favor with the royal couple. But Isabella had hopes of elevating the Spanish court; she knew that the royal environment would influence the culture of the country.

Isabella's formal education, along with her background and training in the arts, was seriously deficient because she had been raised in exile by her mother, who was her principal source of knowledge. Isabella compensated by placing added emphasis on improvement of the arts, humanities, and scholastic achievement in Spain. She began collecting books. In her *alcázar* at Segovia she eventually collected more than 250 volumes, including the Scriptures and other religious works, histories of Spain, volumes on Greek and Roman history and philosophy, Spanish law books, works on medicine and astrology, and even guides to hawking and hunting — two of Ferdinand's favorite pastimes. There were also volumes of Spanish and French songs, Spanish poetry, the tales of King Arthur, Virgil's *Aeneid*, and even the ribald works of Boccaccio, the Italian author of the *Decameron*.

Where Isabella inspired both respect and love in Castile, Ferdinand inspired only respect. . . . But he had the great virtue of being successful, and this brought its own reward in loyalty. . . . He was a man in a man's world and could command an obediance that Isabella alone might have found impossible to enforce.
—MELVEENA MCKENDRICK
biographer

Ferdinand was the driving force behind Spain's foreign policy. The king survived his wife by 12 years, during which time he fought to retain control of Castile and plotted to establish Spanish power in the Italian peninsula.

This book, which contains the first reference to blood circulation, was among the earliest to be printed in Spain. Isabella encouraged the secular scholarship of the Renaissance, even hiring humanist tutors for her own children.

Isabella tried to provide for all her children the things she had lacked. She brought to her court people of great learning, such as the Italian humanists Antonio and Alessandro Geraldini, Lucio Marineo, and Pietro Martire d'Anghiera (known to the Spaniards as Pedro Mártir) to tutor her children in philosophy and theology. Juana became fluent in Latin and was a skilled musician. The chief tutor to Prince John was the eminent scholar Diego de Deza. Isabella's youngest daughter, Catherine, as the wife of Henry VIII of England, would be known throughout Europe as "a miracle of feminine learning" and would champion the cause of female education, at the time a revolutionary concept.

Yet, despite such apparent "enlightenment," the court of Spain still observed many customary rites, including the Renaissance practice of "courtly love," in which married couples often looked outside their bond to experience a "higher," unattainable love. Ferdinand had a number of short-lived love affairs with other women at court. Isabella knew about them but dismissed them as unimportant. It was expected that monarchs would not let affairs of the heart interfere with the affairs of state; neither Ferdinand nor Isabella ever seriously jeopardized their relationship.

Isabella and Ferdinand engaged in many activities meant to broaden their own horizons. The king loved to ride horseback and hunt, while the queen spent hours in prayer. Isabella also spent a great

The architecture of the College of San Gregorio, Valladolid, shows Moorish influence. Ferdinand and Isabella founded universities throughout Spain to improve national education.

deal of time sewing and embroidering with her ladies-in-waiting, a common pastime for noblewomen. And neither monarch ever lacked for companionship. By 1497 there were 1,100 people in attendance at court, and they were almost always on the move. Royal courts were established in alcázars all over the country. These palaces were often breathtaking to behold from the outside — magnificent, sprawling stone structures of massive proportions. Yet the interiors were strikingly stark, no doubt because each was used perhaps once every five or six years, so there was no point in spending extravagant sums of money on furnishings. In all probability, each also reflected Isabella's prudent and austere upbringing. The exception was the al-

In 1493 King Charles VIII of France restored captured territories to Aragon in return for Ferdinand's pledge not to aid certain Italian states. Charles, however, would be outsmarted by Ferdinand's devious diplomacy.

CAROLVS VIII GALREX

cázar at Soria in Old Castile, which was the home of their only son and heir, Prince John. This castle was furnished lavishly — the obvious effort of two doting parents who wanted to make sure their son lacked nothing.

Isabella was no less enthusiastic about national education. When Paris outlawed the use of the recently invented printing press (first used in Europe in the 1450s), Isabella encouraged its use in Spain in order to increase the number of books available. Furthermore, all duties paid on imported books were removed. Higher education thrived; the University of Salamanca, in western Castile, was staffed with renowned scholars and became one of the leading centers of education in Europe.

In 1497 Cisneros, acting on Isabella's instructions, commissioned the Spanish architect Pedro de Gumiel to design and build a new university at Alcalá de Henares. The school became a monument to Isabella, for it had a number of women on its faculty, and eventually, after Isabella's death, made education available not only to the nobility but to many others on a much broader base.

After royal power in Spain had been consolidated, Ferdinand turned his attention to foreign policy and Aragonese interests. The cornerstone of Ferdinand's foreign policy was expansion; he wanted to establish Spain as a respected force in the wider arena of European politics. In 1493 he signed a treaty with Charles VIII of France that granted to Aragon the small regions of Roussillon and Cerdagne, over which France and Aragon had been in conflict since his father's reign. In return, Ferdinand promised not to form an alliance with any country that was France's enemy, with the exception of the papal states. A year later, France invaded Italy, and by early 1495 Charles's troops occupied Rome and Naples.

Ferdinand had vested interests in Italy — he was himself the king of Sicily — and his family had ruled Naples for more than 50 years. Moreover, because Italy was not a united nation but a collection of independent states, Ferdinand saw it as the perfect

An early-16th-century Spanish knight. Through a diplomatic loophole Ferdinand was able to free himself from his agreement with France. He immediately sent troops to Italy to fight the invading French.

For Spanish aid against Charles VIII, whose army had captured Rome, Pope Alexander VI conferred the title *los reyes católicos* — the Catholic Monarchs — on Ferdinand and Isabella.

area to establish Spanish power. He immediately broke the treaty with France through a clever loophole. "The kingdom of Naples is a fief of the church," he declared to the outraged Charles. "Therefore, my duty toward Naples must come before my obligation to France." With this declaration, Ferdinand showed himself to be a sly, devious diplomat and politician. Although Ferdinand was only looking out for his own interests, Pope Alexander VI viewed Spain as his defender and conferred upon Ferdinand and Isabella the title they proudly bore for the rest of their lives: *los reyes católicos* — the Catholic monarchs.

Ferdinand ordered troops sent from Sicily into the Italian mainland to free Naples. Under the brilliant leadership of Gonzalo de Córdoba, the Spanish army quickly won back Naples and freed Rome. In 1498 a peace treaty was concluded with France. The conflict in Italy, however, would soon be renewed under the new French king, Louis XII, who came to the throne that same year.

Having worked so hard to consolidate Spain internally, Isabella and Ferdinand now began to devise ways to extend Spanish influence in Europe through diplomacy. By designing a series of marriages between their children and the offspring of the great rulers of Europe, the Catholic monarchs sought to create political alliances that would ensure the future power of Spain. The broad aim of their dynastic policy was the encirclement and isolation of France, which threatened to become the single strongest power on the continent. In 1490 Isabella, their morbid, frail (probably tubercular) eldest daughter, had been married to Alfonso of Portugal, the heir to the throne. Queen Isabella, whose mother had been Portuguese, had always dreamed of seeing one of her daughters on the throne of Spain's neighbor, and such a union would serve to lessen any hostilities that might arise between the two countries. Eight months after the marriage, however, Alfonso was killed in a riding accident, and Isabella returned home to observe four years of mourning.

Holy Roman Emperor and Habsburg king Maximilian I ruled a vast amount of land in Europe. In a dynastic coup Ferdinand and Isabella arranged marriages for two of their children to the Habsburg house.

In 1495 Alfonso's uncle Manuel became king and asked for Isabella's hand. Although she at first refused, Isabella was convinced by her mother to accept, but she did so only on two conditions: first, that all the Jews be expelled from Portugal (she was as blindly devoted to her religion as her mother), and second, that she and Manuel be married in a very quiet ceremony. Manuel, anxious to win this political plum, agreed readily, and in 1497 young Isabella finally became queen of Portugal.

In the meantime, Ferdinand had made several more arrangements. In a diplomatic coup, marriages were arranged with two of the Habsburg imperial children. Prince John, the heir to the throne of Spain, would marry Princess Margaret, daughter of Holy Roman Emperor Maximilian I, who had sought a Spanish alliance since 1488. Union with the Habsburg empire was especially attractive to Ferdinand and Isabella because its lands — Austria, the German states, Burgundy, and the Netherlands — encircled France. Their intelligent but nervous daughter Juana was betrothed to Philip, who was the real prize among the emperor's children, for in addition to being the most handsome prince in Europe, he was also heir to the thrones of Burgundy and Austria.

In 1496, Juana, not quite 17 years of age, sailed north to marry Philip the Handsome. A few months later the ship returned to Spain carrying Princess Margaret, who married Prince John in 1497. At the same time, arrangements were made to have Catherine, Ferdinand and Isabella's youngest child, mar-

Maximilian's son, Philip, called "the Handsome," stood to inherit the throne of Austria and Burgundy and was a possible candidate to succeed his father as Holy Roman Emperor.

Ferdinand and Isabella's daughter Juana married Philip the Handsome in 1496. To their dismay the Spanish monarchs soon discovered that Juana's jealous love for her unfaithful husband was driving her insane. She would be known as *la Loca*—the Mad.

ried to Arthur, heir to the throne of Henry VII, king of England. These brilliant and politically astute marriages must have been the envy of all Europe. No one could have foreseen that such great plans would soon turn to ashes.

In October 1497, as Ferdinand and Isabella attended the wedding of their daughter Isabella to Manuel, Prince John fell desperately ill. Ferdinand sped to his son's side, arriving just in time to see him die. The king and queen were shattered by his death, for he had been the only one who could have inherited the crowns of both Aragon and Castile. Attention turned to Margaret, Prince John's widow, who was pregnant; a male child would keep alive the dream of a prince to rule over a unified Spain. But a few months later the baby was stillborn.

Catherine of Aragon, the monarchs' youngest daughter, was betrothed to the crown prince of England. In 1501 Catherine left Spain for her new home, but Isabella, under intense emotional stress over Juana, was too weak to see her off.

The troubles of the unhappy king and queen had not yet ended. Upon receiving word that John had died, Philip immediately proclaimed himself and his wife, Juana, heirs to the throne of Castile. Aside from the fact that Juana's older sister, Isabella, was the rightful heir to Castile, Queen Isabella realized that Philip — vain, selfish, and a Francophile (a lover of the French and their culture) — would be a disastrous ruler in Spain. Daughter Isabella, now queen of Portugal, was expecting a child, and her parents fervently hoped it would be a boy. In August 1498 Isabella bore a son, Miguel, but she died shortly after the delivery. Her son, although given loving care in Spain, would die within two years. Within a short space of time, the royal couple had lost two children and two grandchildren, and their dream of having an heir who could become king of a united Spain had all but vanished.

In 1500 King Manuel asked for the hand of Maria, the monarchs' only remaining unbetrothed daughter, and they consented. The king and queen then sent for Philip and Juana, who had had a son, Charles. Because her elder sister had died, Juana was now legal heir to the throne of Castile and therefore was required to receive the nobles' oath of loyalty. No doubt Ferdinand wanted them to bring young Charles with them so he could influence his grandson, for Charles was heir not only to the Habsburg lands of Austria and Burgundy and a possible candidate for Holy Roman emperor, but stood to inherit all of Spain as well. Philip and Juana came to Spain, but much to Ferdinand's chagrin, Charles remained at home.

Ferdinand and Isabella were unprepared for the change in their daughter. Juana had always been a sensitive, nervous child. It was clear now that she was madly, pathologically, in love with Philip; he was totally indifferent to her. Although Juana was pregnant with their second child, Philip soon found an excuse to return home without her, leaving her to stay with her parents until the baby was born. Ferdinand, their second son, was born a few months later, but in the meantime Juana had become obsessed over her longing for Philip. Her behavior became irrational; at one point she ran from the castle in her nightgown and clung to a castle fence for a full day and night, resisting all efforts to calm her down. Isabella finally managed to get her inside, but by then the news had spread, and Juana had been dubbed "Juana la Loca"—Juana the Mad.

The trial of having to deal with Juana and the deaths of her hopes for Spain began to take their toll on Isabella. The queen grew weaker and weaker; she was too frail even to escort Catherine to the border of Spain in 1501 for her voyage to England. Sadly, she was never to see her daughter again, nor was she to know the tragedy that ensued, for Arthur died shortly after the marriage, and Catherine married Henry VIII, a union that was to end in bitter divorce in 1533.

After Catherine's young husband died, she was betrothed to his brother, Henry. Catherine would be the first of the six wives of King Henry VIII of England; he divorced her in 1533.

The Habsburg prince Charles, eldest son of Juana and Philip, was first in line to inherit the combined Spanish kingdoms. It was a bitter realization for Isabella, who wanted to see a native Spaniard rule her beloved country.

The only successful marriage among the Spanish royal children was that of Maria to Manuel; in a cruel twist of fate, although they had eight children, none was successor to the Spanish throne. That privilege belonged to Prince Charles of Austria, who, upon his election as Holy Roman Emperor Charles V in 1519, would rule over more of Europe than anyone since Charlemagne had in the 9th century.

In July 1504 both Ferdinand and Isabella fell ill. Ferdinand recovered quickly, but Isabella did not. For three months she struggled desperately to regain her strength, but to no avail. On October 12, 1504, realizing her condition, she wrote her will, naming Juana her legal heir. But knowing Juana's unstable mental condition, she appointed Ferdinand regent of Castile until her grandson Charles came of age. In her will the queen specified that she be buried with her husband upon his death so that "our bodies may symbolize and enjoy beneath the ground the close relationship that was ours when we were alive." On November 26, 1504, Isabella died. Pedro Mártir, the Italian historian who served as a diplomatic representative at the Spanish court, wrote, "My hand falls powerless by my side, for very sorrow. The world has lost its noblest ornament." From Medina del Campo, where she died, Isabella was borne through dark, driving torrents of rain south to Granada, the scene of her greatest triumph, where she was laid to rest in the royal tomb.

Ferdinand now faced the struggle of keeping control of Castile. The Castilian nobles did not trust him, so they asked Philip the Handsome to come and rule in place of his disturbed wife, Juana. Ferdinand decided, somewhat cynically, that the only way to retain power was to have a son, and so he decided to remarry. He chose for his wife Germaine, niece of Louis XII of France. Nonetheless, Philip accepted the nobles' invitation, and in 1506 he came to Castile to rule, but within two months he unexpectedly died. This final blow drove Juana into complete insanity. She refused to allow Philip to be buried and carted his body around for two years. Finally, Ferdinand had her locked up, with Philip's corpse, in a fortress at Tordesillas. She was 29 when Ferdinand confined her; she died at the age of 76, still at Tordesillas, but her dead husband had been taken from her in 1525 to be laid to rest in Granada. Juana would join him there in 1555.

With Philip dead and Juana incapable of ruling, Ferdinand reclaimed the Castilian throne as regent. The fanatical Cisneros, still seeking to promote the true religion, managed to talk the king into launching a crusade in North Africa to expel the Moors. But Ferdinand lacked Isabella's religious fervor, and although he did savor war, he had no heart for a religious campaign; he was more interested in Italy.

Ferdinand lived for 12 years following the death of Isabella. He spent much of that time embroiled in a series of political maneuvers and intrigues among the powers of Europe for control in Italy. In 1503 the Spanish had taken Naples from the French for the second time, and a year later Ferdinand acquired the title king of Naples, which he held until

> *To this last great effort—the wise marriage of their children; the weaving of a strong dynastic net—Isabel[la] devoted the closing years of her life. And if she failed in it, she failed only through the twists of scandals and destinies.*
> —TOWNSEND MILLER
> historian

The statues of Ferdinand and Isabella at the royal tomb in Granada show them in a typically devout posture. When Isabella died in 1504, Ferdinand lost the support of much of the Castilian nobility, whose primary loyalty had always been to Isabella.

his death. In 1508 an alliance was formed among Spain, France, the papal states, and Emperor Maximilian to conquer and subdivide the wealthy republic of Venice. Ferdinand won several Italian cities from this adventure. In 1512 Ferdinand invaded Navarre, took Pamplona, its capital, and ultimately incorporated all of the small kingdom into Aragon. Ferdinand would spend much of the rest of his life plotting new but ultimately fruitless ways to acquire more territory in Italy.

Ferdinand developed a dislike for his oldest grandson, Charles, who was being raised and educated as a Habsburg. He tried to orchestrate a scheme in which his grandson Ferdinand, Charles's brother, who had been born and raised in Spain, would become heir to everything if Germaine did not have a son. Ferdinand and Germaine did have a son, but

the infant died almost immediately after birth. Fate seemed to thwart all of the dynastic plans of the Catholic monarchs.

In January 1516 Ferdinand fell ill, perhaps of a heart attack. When it became clear he was dying, he was persuaded to draw up a final will (he had written several) in which he named regents for Spain. In Aragon he made regent his illegitimate son Alonso, the archbishop of Saragossa; Castile came under the regency of Cisneros. The title of king would pass to Ferdinand's grandson Charles when he came of age. For poor Juana, still imprisoned in the bleak castle of Tordesillas, Ferdinand left only instructions that she not be told of his death. On January 23, 1516, the king of Aragon died at the age of 63. According to his wishes, he was buried in Granada with Isabella.

8

The Legacy of the Catholic Kings

On September 17, 1517, 17-year-old Charles arrived in Spain to claim the crowns of Aragon and Castile. He saw before him a unified country, something no Spanish monarch had beheld for more than 800 years. Ferdinand and Isabella had made their dream of unification a reality, but their fervent wish that the country be ruled by a Spaniard, by a native son who would cherish the land as they had, remained unfulfilled. Charles, brought up in Flanders, was a Habsburg prince; his interests extended far beyond the borders of Spain.

Through Ferdinand's diplomacy, Spain had established itself in the international arena with embassies in virtually every European country. It maintained a standing army second to none. It enjoyed supremacy on the sea and was developing an armada to equal its land army. Furthermore, the results of Columbus's voyages west (he made four) would ultimately go beyond the adventurer's own visionary expectations. Spanish explorers would discover and claim new lands throughout the Western Hemisphere; Diego Velázquez took Venezuela (1500) and Cuba (1511); Hernando Cortés conquered the Aztecs in Mexico in 1521. The following year, Spanish ships under the command of Ferdinand Magellan, a Portuguese nobleman in the service of Spain, completed a circle around the globe.

Both monarchs, especially Isabella, saw the . . . glorious vision of an expanding, crusading Spain.
—MELVEENA MCKENDRICK
biographer

Charles (shown here as emperor) became king of Spain in 1516 when Ferdinand died. Although he spent much of his life in Spain, Charles was always more concerned with the Holy Roman Empire and saw Ferdinand and Isabella's kingdom as only a peripheral part of his realm.

Columbus sets foot in the New World, 1492. The discovery of the Americas, to which Columbus made three more journeys, greatly enriched Spain, but Spanish sea power would not outlast the 16th century.

The *conquistadores* of Francisco Pizarro overcame the Inca civilization of Peru in 1532. Juan Ponce de León, Francisco Coronado, and Hernando de Soto explored the interior of the North American continent. Spain, spurred on by an influx of golden treasures and tales of untold riches in the new lands, became a leader in the Age of Exploration. The crown retained control of trade from the Americas and took one-fifth of the gold and silver mined there in taxes, a policy that greatly increased the wealth and power of the monarchy.

But the accomplishments of Ferdinand and Isabella go much deeper than the external signs of a powerful country. Through the vision of the Catholic monarchs, a sense of national identity began to take hold in Spain. The Spanish would no longer be fragmented into hundreds of small communities, each arbitrarily ruled by a local nobleman, but would find themselves held together by common bonds forged by the Catholic monarchs.

Isabella and Ferdinand also left a dark side to their legacy; the Spanish Inquisition, religious intolerance, and a narrowness of viewpoint left them at times on the fringe of European politics. These were self-limiting boundaries. In the two centuries that followed, while the rest of Europe flourished, Spain made little progress. The Inquisition sank deep roots and continued to blight Spanish history until it was abolished in 1834. After the initial wealth of the Americas was exhausted, Spanish control began to wane. Its mastery of the seas was contested and eventually overcome; the disastrous defeat of Spain's fleet in 1588 signaled the rise of England as the dominant force at sea. Spain proved immune to the spreading Protestant Reformation and afforded little fertile ground for the liberal, rational ideas of the 18th-century Enlightenment to take hold. What does remain in the legacy of Ferdinand and Isabella is a love for and pride in Spain as a nation; it is this deep feeling for their country and the desire to see it achieve its greatness that over the centuries has endeared the Catholic monarchs to the Spanish people.

In Granada Ferdinand and Isabella (left) lie entombed next to the unfortunate Philip and Juana. The Catholic Monarchs stipulated in their wills that they were to be buried together so that they would be as close in death as they had been in life.

Further Reading

Berger, Josef. *Discoverers of the New World.* New York: American Heritage, 1960.
Fernandez-Armesto, Felipe. *Ferdinand and Isabella.* New York: Taplinger, 1975.
McKendrick, Melveena. *Ferdinand and Isabella.* New York: Harper & Row, 1968.
Miller, Townsend. *The Castles and the Crown.* New York: Coward-McCann, Inc., 1963.
Rowdon, Maurice. *The Spanish Terror.* New York: St. Martin's Press, 1974.

Chronology

1451	Isabella born to John II of Castile and Isabella of Portugal
1452	Ferdinand born to King John II of Aragon and Juana Enriquez
1460	Ferdinand ascends to the throne of Aragon
Oct. 1469	Ferdinand marries Isabella at Valladolid
1470	Isabella's first child, Isabella, is born
1472	Ferdinand proclaimed heir to the Spanish throne
1474	King Henry IV dies without an heir; Isabella proclaims herself queen of Castile
1475	Henry's daughter Juana la Beltraneja lays claim to the throne; Portugal invades Castile, led by Alfonso V, Juana's suitor
1476	Ferdinand's army massacres the Portuguese at Toro Isabella nominates Ferdinand as grand master of the Santiago Knights
1478	Ferdinand and Isabella's only son, John, is born Roman Catholic church organizes the Spanish Inquisition Granada refuses to pay its yearly tribute to the crown
1479	Ferdinand and Isabella's third child, Juana, is born Spanish forces defeat Alfonso of Portugal
1480	Ferdinand and Isabella assemble the Cortes (parliament)
1481	War to regain possession of Granada begins
1482	Marques of Cádiz attacks Alhama Ferdinand attacks Loja unsuccessfully and is saved by Cádiz
1485	Ferdinand takes Ronda, a fortress, and Loja
1487	Siege of Málaga; Moors agree to an unconditional surrender
1489	Spanish assault on Baza
1492	Columbus discovers the New World Heightened oppression of Jews in Spain Ferdinand and Isabella issue an edict stating that all non-Christians must either convert or leave Spain Juan de Canamas tries to assassinate Ferdinand
1495	Cisneros becomes archbishop; with Isabella advocates religious homogeneity for Spain Monastic orders are reformed
1496	Juana marries Philip the Handsome, a Habsburg prince
1497	Son John dies; Philip proclaims himself and Juana rulers of Castile
1500	Diego Velázquez claims Venezuela for Spain
1503	Spain takes Naples from France
1504	Isabella dies
1511	Velázquez takes Cuba
1516	Ferdinand dies

Index

Paul Stevens is a former English instructor and is currently a free-lance writer living in Michigan.

Arthur M. Schlesinger, jr., taught history at Harvard for many years and is currently Albert Schweitzer Professor of the Humanities at City University of New York. He is the author of numerous highly praised works in American history and has twice been awarded the Pulitzer Prize. He served in the White House as special assistant to Presidents Kennedy and Johnson.

PICTURE CREDITS